Praise for
The Gamechanger's Playbook

"Tisha recognizes how well-positioned our industry is to meet the demand for more energy while also reducing environmental impact. She has charted a playbook for the game-changing leadership we need to move beyond polarization to achieve our shared aspirations for a clean energy future."

—Alan Armstrong, president and chief executive officer, Williams Companies

"Tisha Schuller is a 'whisperer' of sorts to executives across the hydrocarbon industry. Her unique perspective helps translate social challenges of the day to meaningful innovation; not short cut innovation, but the bolder kind that uses combinations of existing components to unlock heightened company performance and connection with stakeholders.

"If you're trying to disrupt or manage the disruption of the status quo, you're not going to do it by playing the game by the old rules. Learning and innovation go hand in hand; success yesterday doesn't ensure success tomorrow. Tisha's honest assessment, combined with her framework for thinking, drives bottom-line results. I find her a tremendous resources and am sure you will as well."

—Suzanne Ogle, CEO and President, Southern Gas Association; President, Gas Machinery Research Council

"Years of market, social and environmental disruption have led the oil and gas industry to understand it's future in ways never contemplated. Thankfully, at this precipice, Tisha Schuller provides us with this insightful and timely examination of how our industry can not just adapt, but thrive in an uncertain future."

—Kevin Krausert, President & CEO, Beaver Drilling Ltd.

"This book describes an essential truth of the oil and gas business—the millennial generation has expectations of us, both as a place to work and as participants in energy transitions. Tisha Schuller reminded me that disruptive leadership is hard work, but taking it on also frees up the leader from just arguing for their place in the energy mix. If you're thinking about the future of your oil and gas job or company—read this book with a highlighter in your hand and take notes. This WILL be on the exam!"

—John Dabbar, Vice President, Federal and State Government Affairs, ConocoPhillips

The Gamechanger's Playbook

HOW OIL & GAS LEADERS THRIVE IN AN ERA OF CONTINUOUS DISRUPTION

Tisha Schuller

The Gamechanger's Playbook
How Oil & Gas Leaders Thrive in an Era of Continuous
Disruption

Copyright 2020 © Tisha Schuller

All rights reserved. No part of this book may be reproduced
in any form or by any electronic or mechanical means, including information storage and retrieval systems, without
written permission from the author, except in the case of a
reviewer, who may quote brief passages embodied in critical
articles or in a review.

Trademarked names may appear throughout this book.
Rather than use a trademark symbol with every occurrence
of a trademarked name, names are used in an editorial
fashion, with no intention of infringement of the respective
owner's trademark.

The information in this book is distributed on an "as is" ba-
sis, without warranty. Although every precaution has been
taken in the preparation of this work, neither the author nor
the publisher shall have any liability to any person or entity
with respect to any loss or damage caused or alleged to be
caused directly or indirectly by the information contained
in this book.

ISBN: 979-8-698-68464-0

For North America's oil and gas workers.
You're the lifeblood of our present and our possibility.

Contents

Foreword

It is all a bit much. There is a wind that flows under everything we do these days. A wind full of all our uncertainty, angst, and loss of the moment. We mostly ignore this wind, because we are leaders—not just of work, but often of our family unit as well as civic organizations— and we think the wind will distract us and threaten our ability to lead if we give it any meaningful attention.

I experienced the impulse to ignore the wind viscerally a few days before writing this, when I asked my husband, Brian, what he thought of our boys' going back to school 100 percent online, and he said: "I make a point of not thinking about it—especially what it means societally." That is it: the apparent necessity of avoiding the pandemic's emotional wind.

There is plenty to do, so the wind is sometimes easy to

ignore. Other times, it is a burgeoning, seeping uncertainty that threatens to bluster into our day. We engage our well-honed discipline, return to our mantle, lead the troops to get done what must be accomplished.

But to do that, we give up something. The disruption of the pandemic has upended our life and the oil and gas industry. But perhaps more importantly, it has created an opening: an opening to do the upending ourselves—to take on the trends setting up in opposition to oil and gas, in opposition to the part we will play in a prosperous, increasingly sustainable energy future. I wrote this book so that we, you and I, don't miss this once-in-a-generation leadership opportunity.

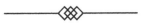

I love the oil and gas industry. It wasn't always that way. When I began my career in the early '90s, I reluctantly did environmental consulting for oil and gas firms, hoping to be, as my uncle who was a groundwater consultant put it, *part of the solution rather than part of the problem.* I made the transition from environmental activist to consultant for the oil and gas industry as part of the normal transition to adulthood, taking on job and family responsibilities as they came.

My transition to serving as the *face of the oil and gas industry,* came later, in 2009, when I thought—that as an environmental scientist and geologist—I could tamp down some of the controversy over fracking by inserting myself into the middle of it as the president and CEO of the Colorado Oil & Gas Association (COGA). That was, one might argue, an unconventional career move.

Leaving my comfortable life as a regional manager for an environmental consulting firm was the least of the challenges involved in that transition. I also had to leave my identity behind. I had been raising my free-range children as your average Boulder mom would—which meant homemade baby food, toys without plastic or batteries, and of course, cloth diapers. The transition was huge, challenging, and—in some cases—dangerous.

Five and half years later, my love affair with the oil and gas industry was solidified. Not, as one longtime friend foreshadowed, because "they must be paying you a lot of money." Instead, my attachment has come from a long path of staying open-minded and flexible to the best information I can get my hands on. As I spent more than five long years at COGA, I constantly asked myself these two questions: (1) Can we get off oil and gas? and (2) Can the oil and gas industry produce more responsibly? The answers to these questions gave me an understanding of the complexity of the energy system, the critical role that oil and gas play around the world in creating our lifestyle and prosperity, and insights into how we in the industry can do better.

The exploration that I began at COGA has continued. In 2015 I left COGA and founded Adamantine Energy, where I have built a team to focus on future-proofing the oil and gas industry. Why would one of the largest and most important industries in the world require future-proofing? Because while it is true that the world requires more and more oil and gas to feed the lifeblood of economies, it is also true our industry now faces unprecedented existential risk on several fronts.

The industry has spent the last several years celebrating the first and fighting the second. At Adamantine, our work has been to conspire for good with industry to chart a new course. We work with the idea that two apparently opposing ideas can also be true at the same time. As the starting place for our work and this book, we will look at these two truths:

- The world needs lots of energy—more than ever before.
- There is growing opposition against nearly all oil and gas development and operation. This opposition is about to become the dominant global mindset as we move into the energy future.

This conundrum presents a huge social risk for oil and gas. It also presents us with an enormous opportunity, an opportunity we don't want to miss—but we will if we continue avoiding the pandemic wind.

By tuning out the pandemic wind, we as leaders put blinders on. We turn down our experiential intuition. And we ignore the very opportunity the energy conundrum offers us. In doing this, we potentially accelerate how the winds of disruption will change everything.

The pandemic and economic upheaval have created an opening—an opening to seize the leadership and meet the desperate desire of the public for leaders to show the way into the future. (Don't you wish someone would come along and please show the way?! It turns out that someone is you.)

The wind is fueled by three disruptors, which I detail in Chapter 2. They were here before the pandemic, but the health and economic upheavals of 2020 have accelerated their disruptions. They have made the world more treacherous, but they have also created a crack for us to jump through. This is perhaps our industry's last best chance to look our disruptors in the eye and respond with a vision for the future, including the energy future. We can lead not only into next year, but the next three decades.

To write this book, I had to look straight into the pandemic wind and ask myself—what am I and what are we so afraid of? There is plenty to fear, as you know. You are already starting to tick a list off in your head. There is a personal list of what is at stake, the company list, the industry list, the community list, the society list… Never you mind. That is the wind again.

I looked straight into the pandemic wind of *what could go wrong, what might never be the same again, what power structures will collapse,* and *what, if anything recognizable will remain?*

There are themes here of general relevance to all civic leaders. But I focused on our industry, the oil and gas industry, because we were particularly vulnerable *before* the pandemic, price collapse, and economic devastation. It seemed our place in the world would continue to shift from heroes to villains. Back then the path to success was unclear, and now it is wickedly so.

So I looked particularly for us—with a keen eye to the millions of men and women who bring oil and gas to market keeping the world energized and every day creating the foundation for whatever the recovery from this situation will look like. I asked myself those questions for our industry—what could go wrong, what might never be the same again, what power structures will collapse, and what, if anything recognizable, will remain? And what can we do to emerge even stronger as these challenges hit full throttle?

Society's response, recovery, and rebuild to the pandemic all need us. And we must rise to the occasion immediately. By mobilizing in this moment, we can do more than secure our place in our society's recovery from the pandemic and rebuilding of the economy. We will define our place in the leadership future for decades to come.

I charted a course to share with you.

01
Why We Must Seize the Energy Future

Plenty of people will object to my central thesis that we in the oil and gas industry must propel ourselves urgently into creating the energy future. After all, many of the trends that I will describe in the next chapter on disruptors are founded in a shifting public opinion that foreshadows doom for our industry. If I were one of those who unabashedly opposed the oil and gas industry (and I was once one of them), I would see this narrative of continued oil and gas leadership as an aggressive attack on the accelerating march to the new energy future.

But they are wrong. We will lead. We simply need to see how.

To guide you there, I am going to thread the needle of one of my favorite themes: *Both of These Things Are True.*

It is true that we in the oil and gas industry can no longer ignore a public who increasingly does not like us, trust us, or value the critical work we do. The turning tide of public opinion has morphed into an existential threat that cannot be ignored.

It is simultaneously true that we—the oil and gas industry—can invent, accelerate, create, and execute on the decarbonized energy future faster, better, and cheaper than any existing agency, organization, or system.

And so if you can't beat them, join them.

Yes, that would go for both sides.

But I'm getting ahead of myself, so allow me to explain and introduce the two mindsets.

It is a bit obnoxious that my epiphany happened while I was sitting on a porch in Costa Rica in the middle of January. I was envisioning how much different my life would be in seven days when I landed in Calgary. I checked the weather app on my phone for good measure: a high of -23 degrees Celsius (it's not much better in Fahrenheit: -10 degrees). Yes, that temperature would certainly feel different. But it was more than that.

Alberta has been and should be one of the world's friendliest environments to conduct the business of oil and gas. Instead, in January of 2019, pipeline companies were facing unprecedented regulatory upheaval and nearly constant project opposition. Why?

The opposition was not just activism. Climate change had become the tent under which all energy conversations were being conducted. In 2018, the heat had turned up in Canada on the climate conversation in a way that even the most reticent oil and gas executive could no longer ignore. Under pressure from public polls, the Canadian government had recently overhauled its pipeline regulatory system in a fashion crushing to the industry. Large oil and gas companies were facing direct shareholder pressure to develop climate threat assessments. And proposed projects in even the friendliest jurisdictions were facing the question: *Why should we approve your project when we should get off oil and gas today?* Oil and gas regulatory approvals were becoming universally mired down in questions and critiques related to climate. And in these conversations, fossils were and are nothing but the fuels of the past.

I was about to travel to Calgary to give a talk to the country's pipeliners at the annual dinner for the Canadian Energy Pipeline Association. I was reflecting upon my already prepared talk, which seemed unlikely to meet what the moment required. Up until this point, my keynote talks followed the theme of my work and book, *Accidentally Adamant*:

- Oil and gas are crucial;
- The public largely doesn't understand how essential oil and gas are to every aspect of social

and economic well-being; and

- Our job in the industry is to educate and engage the public more thoughtfully.

My talk was well traveled and had passed the industry audience enthusiasm test with flying colors. The first two parts of the talk helped all of us in oil and gas feel better about the situation we found ourselves in, and the third focused on what we needed to do better. While there was clearly a lot we can do better, it was becoming increasingly clear that engaging and educating the public was no longer sufficient. Certainly, it wasn't solving the challenges in Alberta. Nor those happening in my home state of Colorado.

"Educate and engage" is still the first line of defense for our industry in the face of opposition. I had extensive firsthand experience in conducting education and out-reach campaigns on behalf of the oil and gas industry. When I first joined COGA, I too thought, *if only they know what we know!* (And, p.s.: who better to tell them than me?!) My first hire at COGA was a researcher, and that first year we made dozens of fact sheets. I hit the road constantly providing educational briefings and science-based narratives around safety, environmental protection, and the importance and complexity of the energy system.

It took years for me to see that education plays a limited role. The science of behavioral economics finally helped me reckon with a public not only dismissive of my pre-sentations but often enraged by them, not calmed. In our polarized world, education is only effective once trust and relationship are established.

I realized that our linear path—to educate and engage about how important oil and gas are in order to promote public acceptance—would no longer suffice.

So then what?

We have done such a good job of creating abundant, affordable, always available energy that the world, including the people around us every day, takes it for granted. Universally, our neighbors, supporters, and critics share the expectations that their heat will kick in when they adjust the thermostat, gas stations will have fuel when they pull in to the pump, and the office lights will never flicker. And all of this will happen at a predictable, affordable price.

Around the world, billions of people are coming to have and expect a middle-class quality of life and its requisite available, affordable, reliable energy. Energy is, in fact, the requisite resource developing economies need to emerge into the middle class—making possible the education and employment that transforms villages, cities, and entire economies.

None of this demand is going away soon.

It is because energy is so ever available and reliable that it has become figuratively invisible, laying the groundwork for a public to believe that they no longer require this energy. It's become as available, affordable, and taken for granted as air.

Which brings us back to the idea that two opposing ideas can be true at the same time. In our reality as leaders of the oil and gas industry, both of these things are true:

- The world requires abundant energy—well into the future—more than ever before.
- There is growing opposition against oil and gas development and operation in all its forms.

This paradox matters because if you work in oil and gas in a place like Calgary or Colorado, you bump up against this contradiction every day. It infiltrates each conversation about energy and the environment in ways that are hard to address directly, because much of the public works under the assumption that we do not need fossil fuels anymore.

A stark example is anyone who wants to "leave it in the ground" while, as my colleague likes to say: "blogging about us on a computer we created using energy we brought you." In other words, still benefiting from omnipresent oil- and gas-based materials and fuels.

I pondered all of this while imagining giving my talk in Calgary in a week. We had been focused exclusively for too long on educating the public on the reality of fossils.

Instead, we needed to ask: *How does an oil and gas company make sense of this world where both of these things are true?*

With little time ahead, I set about revising my talk. In the end, I rethought our entire approach to engaging with an increasingly skeptical, hostile public.

We find ourselves at a tipping point for oil and gas social risk. When I refer to social risk, I mean the political, regulatory, and community risk that could delay or threaten your company's project or operations. We have increasingly seen how the public's anger toward oil and gas materially impedes everything from pipeline construction to utility pipe replacement.

We begin with the recognition that a new dichotomy demands a new conversation. The oil and gas industry must increasingly engage with skeptical (or even hostile) individuals who hold decision-making authority. These individuals are looking to a different energy future—one that is high tech, decarbonized, and environmentally sustainable. We cannot meaningfully influence these conversations if we are not participating in them.

As with all mind-bending problems, our approach must be, *seek first to understand*. In the context of the energy future, there are two general mindsets. Let's take a look. Let's begin with *our* mindset. Most of us working in oil and gas have a deep appreciation for two energy realities.

The first reality: We recognize that energy is the lifeblood of our prosperous lives. We have, in fact, done such a good job of producing it that everyone takes it completely for granted. It empowers every aspect of our lives so well that we have almost no tolerance for any disruption. Even an hour without our gadgets charged disorients us mightily! The public is exceptionally sensitive to any price increase at the pump or our home energy bills—and have come to expect energy that is always available, always affordable, and always reliable.

Further, we recognize that energy is nearly the *literal* lifeblood of the global economy, moving goods and services around the world. The public thinks immediately about gasoline for family transportation. But we know that natural gas, diesel, and jet fuel create the lifeblood of economies. So much so that even during a global pandemic, you can go to your local Canadian Tire or Walmart and find nearly anything your heart desires. These fuels are mission critical, and we do not yet have a viable alternative to keep goods and services moving around the globe.

The second reality we in the industry know: The world is going to need more energy. And a lot of it. We know that the most important thing we can do to improve outcomes for developing economies is provide energy. Access to energy in a village, city, or country improves all of the outcomes we care about: reducing infant mortality, lowering birth rates, increasing life expectancy, and improving education levels. For an economy to move its citizens into the middle class, it must be able to industrialize, creating jobs at scale. And this requires industrial-strength energy.

Further, we recognize that oil and gas provide feedstock for all kinds of life-critical things: fertilizer for growing populations, chemicals for development of plastics and electronics, and direct heat for the manufacturing of things like steel or cell phones.

In addition to literally empowering our way of life, this energy will allow billions of people around the world to move toward a prosperous middle-class life. And that is something to celebrate! As a result, nearly 100 percent of new demand will come from developing economies. And this demand will require more oil and gas for the foreseeable future.

So, to summarize our mindset: Energy is the lifeblood of our prosperous lives, and the world is going to demand more and more energy. We must recognize the complexity of the energy system and the reality of energy demand as we engage in any conversation about energy and the environment.

Then there is this other, growing perspective. Let's call it the "fossil-free mindset." This new mindset can seem a mystery, and throughout this book I am going to explain why we can't dismiss it, nor educate people out of it, and how it's rapidly becoming our biggest risk.

I have some insight into this worldview—I live in and am

surrounded by this mindset in Boulder, Colorado. This view holds that climate change presents a *moral obligation* to stop using fossils. (The *moral* part is important, because a conversation about energy and the environment quickly leaves the territory of science and facts, which we all like to pretend is where we are operating from—and instead moves into political identity.) From the perspective of this mindset, it is fine that we need to get off fossil fuels, because we should already be there. And—the holder of this viewpoint argues—we would be, if only we were not manipulated by those greedy companies and the politicians they control.

As we will explore in Chapter 2, we have to study the "fossil-free" mindset because it has moved beyond the Boulders, Berkeleys, and Portlands of the world to occupy and even dominate investor briefings, boardroom strategy sessions, and state legislatures red and blue. In fact, it has traveled to all the venues we used to think we could rely upon to stay pragmatic about energy.

This direction of travel from activist edge to mainstream is a direct result of the three disruptors we will explore in Chapter 2. Oil and gas executives have experienced this shift as their once loyal children went to college and came back ready to go into the work force… *changed*. We have been increasingly surprised as climate began to infiltrate investor analysis, regulatory guidance, and permitting conditions. "Fossil-free" has reached a cultural tipping point. It has arguably already become the dominant mindset—and will solidify that position as North America's demographics continue to shift.

.

Now, I want to acknowledge that this mindset is under-pinned by a kind of magical thinking—one that does not meaningfully acknowledge the demand for and complexities of our energy system. Nevertheless, this worldview is driving real pressure that threatens the further production and use of oil and gas. In the past, we have dismissed or lectured those with these beliefs—but we need to recognize those days are over. The fossil-free mindset is growing rapidly in influence driven by po-litical identity and deep-seated fears beyond objectivity and reason. We do not have to agree, but we do have to understand this perspective—so that we can understand its existential risk for our industry, be more skillful in engaging it, and ultimately lead in alignment with it.

To summarize the fossil-free worldview: Climate change is happening and addressing it is a priority; it is our moral responsibility to stop using fossil fuels. In the shorthand of this perspective, fossils are over.

At the same time our need for oil and gas continues.

Accepting the idea that *both of these things are true* is daunting. But it provides a strong foundation for prepar-ing to lead during overwhelming disruption.

And lead we must. The dueling mindsets have created a vast leadership vacuum. The public wants prosperity, growth, and an ever-improving quality of life—and no one wants to give anything up for it. So who will take them to the energy future they imagine?

People thought that solar panels on rooftops or wind farms in the Midwest were going to solve all our energy problems. People are going to find out: For what they can do, these solutions are too fragmented, too dispersed, and ultimately too small scale. They cannot provide the leadership that this energy moment requires.

Only our industry can work at the level of innovation, investment, and scale required.

We are going to spend Chapter 2 looking at the three disruptors that have created this risk to everything we know about our business and the energy future. You can unleash your skepticism there about: (1) whether we really are at this moment, (2) if only *they* understood the complexity and reality of the energy system, they would support us, and (3) if eventually *they* will understand. We will cover that ground—and after you read through the three disruptors, I believe you will join me in thinking, *Wow, something has got to change.*

Yes. And it's us. We have got to change.

Our industry transformed the world, in nearly every conceivable way. Historians can trace every innovation, every improvement in quality of life, every medical breakthrough—back to a fuel or feedstock that oil and gas made possible. It would have been nice to have a few more decades to savor our successes and bask in public appreciation. I do not need to tell *you* how important our industry has been, is, and will be. But we do not have time for that with the disruptors closing in fast.

Every leading industry has faced juncture points where it must transform itself to maintain its leadership. Industries—including ours—have been doing so through wars, innovations, price collapses, supply disruptions, and superstorms. We have gone from peak oil within sight to peak demand on the horizon within one decade.

We know that no industry will look in 30 years the way it does today. It is just that we had hoped ours would mostly look the same. After all, to invest in those megaprojects to keep the fuel available and affordable, we had to. Personally, I think we will still need some of those megaprojects—but that doesn't change the fact that we have to look at the macro disruptors underway *right now* and think in terms of a massive paradigm shift in how we do business and create the energy future.

Nostalgia is a self-indulgence we can no longer afford. Even adaption is inadequate. We must lead or prepare to die. There is not an oil and gas industry leader I know who would expect—or even want—someone else to re-imagine our industry's future.

(So far that hasn't gone so well, either.)

Everything about this time is deeply unsettling. While identifying the three disruptors helps make sense of the new dynamics we face, it does not get to that deep internal switch each of us needs to flip to become the insightful leader that this moment requires. The disruptors are trends that will persist and wear grooves into ruts and then into canyons that we cannot ignore.

The transition required is first and foremost an individual decision. First, we resolve to face the massive changes underway. Then we assess with raw honesty what they mean for our business, our industry, and our place in the energy future. With such a stark assessment, we can then unravel what the moment requires of us to adapt for survival—but more importantly—to lead to higher ground. And then on to greener pastures.

At each historic, transformative junction of oil and gas leaders, those leaders stood on a great precipice of disruption, risk, and the unknown, just as we do. Once we understand what we must do, we can turn to three timeless values that business leaders have relied on for generations. That is the work of Chapter 3. In times of never-ending turbulence, these values are stable. They are well known to us as leaders and harken to an earlier time to which we can relate.

But the three values do not take us into the past. Embodying them can only lead into the future. A world upside down requires each of us to become dynamic leaders who look around at what has been disrupted and use exactly that disruption to craft a strategy into the energy future. Transitioning away from being disrupted to *being the disruptor* is the strategy of a gamechanger.

In the fourth chapter, we will look at how to flip disruption on its head by harnessing three gamechangers. Although rooted in timeless values, the gamechangers are novel, because they will imagine the energy future, which of course is nothing like anything anyone has ever seen.

Let's go build the energy future.

———◇◇◇———

02

The Three Disruptors

The COVID-19 pandemic did not create any of the disruptors. It did not even directly accelerate any of the disruptors specifically relevant to the oil and gas industry. Instead, the pandemic created a brittle world in which disruptors are magnified—especially three disruptors with which we must reckon immediately:

1. **Rise of the millennials**—your greatest opportunity *and* social risk;

2. **Activism's efficacy**—the anti-oil and -gas ripple tips into mainstream expectations; and

3. **Racial equity & justice**—the societal expectation that we will address them and never go backwards.

We will look at the trends behind each disruptor, how these trends will play out for our industry, in what ways they upset our status quo thinking, and where we should go from here. This chapter is *unsettling*. It is page after page on the disruption of the world as we know it (and perhaps as we wish it could have stayed). We have got to look at the facts head on so we can skillfully craft a path forward. That path will be charted in the decidedly brighter chapters which follow.

Disruptor 1: Rise of the Millennials
Millennials as Your Greatest Opportunity & Your Greatest Social Risk

Without our really noticing, the millennial generation has become the greatest social force since the baby boomers came of age. From now through at least 2050, this cohort is poised to dwarf every other generation in raw numbers (see Figure 1). Millennials—born between 1981 and 1996—are now between 24 and 39 years old and no longer the upstart generation our clichés would have us believe. In fact, this generation is moving into their civic, economic, political, and workforce prime. You may not yet have noticed, but increasingly they dominate the ranks of our employees, investors, regulators, elected officials, and community leaders.

The millennial generation has become the most relevant generation to oil and gas leaders because:

- They dominate the population in raw numbers;
- They are hitting their prime in civic, political, and business leadership;
- They are notably left-leaning politically;
- They are more concerned about both climate and oil and gas than prior generations;
- They are skeptical of businesses; and
- They are the future of our work force.

Figure 1: Population Projections by Age Group [1]

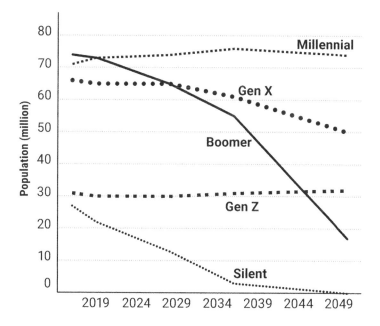

The Disruption: A Demographic Tsunami

There are many good reasons to care about this generation, but I am going to focus on the risk their rise poses to business-as-usual for the oil and gas industry. Risk is a powerful motivator.

In the United States, political affiliation is tied to both concern about climate and opposition to oil and gas development. In the U.S. population at large, there are an increasing number of voters who are Democrats or lean Democratic (we will cover this more in the next disruptor as well).[2] Millennials now match baby boomers in the number of eligible voters, so it is particularly relevant that millennials are significantly more likely to lean Democratic than previous generations (see Figure 2).[3]

Figure 2: Political Party Affiliation for Millennials versus Baby Boomers (Miles, 2020) [4]

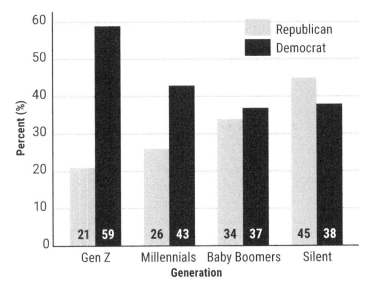

There are, of course, conservative millennials. But even when conservative, millennials are more likely to express concern over climate change and opposition to oil and gas development (see Figure 3).[5]

Figure 3: American Perspective by Generation [6]

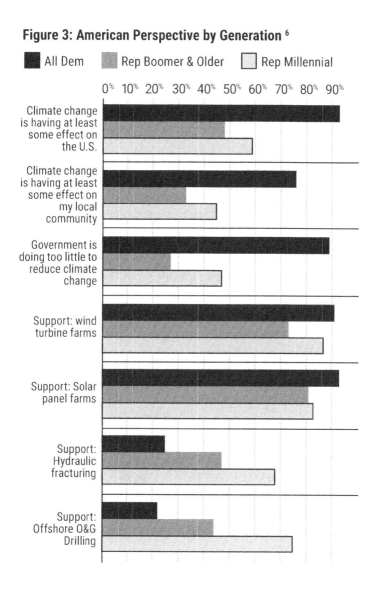

Further, millennials engage with politics and business differently than previous generations. As a cohort, only 25 percent trust big businesses.[7] Millennials are skeptical of the motives of businesses and do not think highly of their impact on society or their trustworthiness.[8] This lack of trust is widespread:

- Seventy-three percent say political leaders are not having a positive impact on the world;
- Forty-five percent have no trust in political leaders for accurate information; and
- Twenty-seven percent do not trust the media.

Millennials base their relationship with businesses on their societal impact, including ethical actions.[9] According to the Deloitte Global Millennial Survey conducted in 2019, millennials deepen their relationships with a business most often based on "its ethical behavior." This is compared with other factors such as a company's political positions, advertising campaigns, or the behavior of its leadership. Interestingly, this relationship moves in both directions. Millennials also *break off* their relationships based on societal impact.

Millennials are also an increasingly important part of our workforces. We can get a two-for-one return on investment by taking the time to understand and engage with this generation: both motivate our work force and transform our relationship with external millennial stakeholders.

The millennial generation has become the most relevant

generation to oil and gas leaders because they dominate population in raw numbers; they are ascending into civic, political, and business leadership; they lean left and are notably concerned about both climate and oil and gas; they are skeptical of businesses in any case; and they are the future of our work force. If you still don't find that package of traits compelling for its risk potential, let's look at how their rise will increasingly and specifically affect our industry.

How the Disruption Is Redefining Oil and Gas

Under a business-as-usual scenario, most millennials can be expected to oppose oil and gas and be concerned about climate. Millennials increasingly dominate relevant leadership roles; therefore, you can expect your interactions with investors, permitting authorities, elected officials, and community leaders to be increasingly informed by millennial opposition to your project and overall climate concern.

Then layer on millennials' distrust of big business. (Regardless of your company's actual size, a millennial stakeholder will certainly consider any oil and gas firm a "big business.")

Without a novel strategy to engage millennials, your relationships with stakeholders across the board can be expected to deteriorate. According to Gallup, once millennial stakeholders become "disengaged," they actively become your opponents.[10] Gallup refers to these stakeholders as "brand destroyers."

We can each feel the political winds underway that are increasing climate as a collective priority. (We will explore this further in Disruptor 2.) As we've discussed, more of the public and therefore our stakeholders aspire to a world where fossil fuels no longer exist—even as they continue to rely on those fuels. This aspiration is becoming mainstream in large part because a new generation— now in their 30s—is entering political and social as well as cultural dominance and driving social discourse.

It does not require a crystal ball to see that our industry's current trajectory and theirs are headed for increasing conflict. Under business as usual, we will lose unless we change our approach. The brand destroyers increasingly have the numbers on their side.

Why Our Conventional Responses & Objections Won't Be Enough

Recognizing the wave of disruption posed by the growing relevance of the millennial generation threatens several areas of conventional thinking. You can think of these areas as our psychological blocks to seeing the threat for what it is. They also form our defensive response to information that is inherently threatening. That does not mean that conventional thinking doesn't have its strengths; after all, it is the way we have always thought about things! These common objections are relevant, important considerations—so let's take them on here:

- We were all liberal when we were young. They are naïve, and they will grow out of it.

- Millennials do not have the experience to wield paradigm-shifting influence on society writ large.

- They are upending the social order and need to wait their turn.

- We set the rules for engagement, not them.

- They are advancing ahead of their time, which is unfair to the generations that came before them.

- They clearly do not understand how hard it is to meet the expectations of our business and our industry.

These are all excellent *conventional* critiques of the millennial wave disruption. I must fight these objections within my own psyche, because as a member of Generation X, I can tell you that *no one* is worrying about what *we* think about fracking or business leadership. (We are the forgotten generation.)

That said, I can tell you from personal experience that it is liberating to embrace the overwhelming data that tell us that millennials are coming into relevance and taking on increasingly impactful leadership roles. They are here. They think what they think. They are changing the world around us *right now*. It does not actually matter at this moment if they are wrong (or right).

We can expect that, as with previous generations, millennials will become more conservative as they age. They will also be burdened by governance, which requires more skill, compromise, and engagement than critiques lobbed from the sidelines. Whether as political or company leaders, they will have to navigate the tradeoffs inherent in executing their responsibilities. And Generation Z will make their lives miserable critiquing how far they have gone off course. (Generation Z has already embarked upon this task with great zeal!)

Personally, I have chosen to embrace the rise of millennials because—to the extent that I think they are right, or wrong, or could look at things differently—my job is to engage, support, and guide the next generation. While that will inevitably *eventually* reduce my relevance and access to power and influence, I can in the meantime participate in shaping a future that is going to happen with or without me.

Where Do We Go from Here?

Everyone facing the three disruptors is already burdened with all their normal leadership responsibilities plus a pandemic. Finding the path forward today is additive to those responsibilities—and the effort is significant. That said, I cannot tell you how much time and energy it frees up to stop fighting the millennial wave and trying to "fix" the oil and gas opposition that comes with it. Embracing this change is empowering. It requires digging deeply into our industry's timeless values, which we will get to in the next chapter.

But first, we have two more disruptors to bravely face.

Disruptor 2: Activism Efficacy
Activism's ripple has tipped into mainstream expectations

Anti-fossil fuel, environmental activism used to be easy to dismiss. It was a fringe movement headquartered on college campuses and influencing only the most liberal enclaves.

No longer.

In the last decade, support for oil and gas has becoming increasingly politically polarized by party and tied to climate change. In many ways, concern over climate has become both (1) a proxy for being liberal, and (2) synonymous with opposition to fossil fuels, including oil and gas and the practice of hydraulic fracturing, or fracking. Even with these ties to political identity, concern over climate is growing among all people in the United States. Further, as we discussed in the previous disruptor, the millennial generation is growing in political relevance, and at the same time increasingly concerned about climate and opposed to oil and gas.

The result is activism gone mainstream. Calls for a "fossil-free energy future" and making "climate a top political and economic priority" are now front and center in any energy conversation. Business, political, regulatory, or community discussions happening anywhere in the country will have climate and decarbonization on the agenda. This has blurred the lines between activism and activities that directly affect your business—such as investor priorities and receiving your project permit approvals.

The Disruption: Activism's Surge to Flood Stage

Concern about climate and prioritization of addressing climate change varies dramatically by party, and this gap has been widening over time. A 2020 poll found that climate change remains a partisan issue nationally, with 88 percent of those who are or lean Democratic saying climate change is a major threat to the United States.[11] Significantly fewer, 31 percent, of those who are or lean Republican respond the same way. Both groups have been increasing steadily over time. The composite of all adults is particularly remarkable: 60 percent view climate as a major threat. Similarly, while U.S. adults are split based on party regarding support for proposals to reduce the use of fossil fuels, a clear majority in the country (60 percent) prefer to decrease them, as shown in Figure 4 opposite.

Activism has moved from the fringe to the mainstream as public opinion has shifted. In this section, we will look at the ripple effects that have made activism the driver of mainstream opposition to oil and gas—which is to say, disrupting the oil and gas business. We will look at how this trend has played out in:

- Pressure from and on investors;
- Aspirational policy, regulations, and legal challenges;
- Directional indicators from the oil and gas majors;

- Divest movement at scale; and

- Pressure from and on the tech sector.

Figure 4: 2019 Americans Who Support the Reduction of Fossil Fuels.[12]

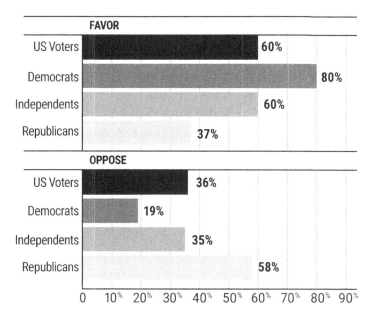

Pressure from and on Investors

For several years we have seen the emergence of environmental-driven investing. Until recently, there were simply small firms or funds within larger firms that focused on environmental social governance (ESG) practices. These were largely boutique-y efforts with good intentions and limited reach. Then seemingly suddenly, in the last year, mainstream investors—some the largest in the world–started making bold statements about their climate and ESG priorities.

Part of this can be attributed to the general shift in public concern about climate, discussed in the previous disruptor. Another can be tied to activism pressure directly on the banks and investment firms.

For example, there has been a focused activist campaign targeting BlackRock called BlackRock's Big Problem. BlackRock is particularly interesting to watch because (1) they are the largest asset manager in the world, and (2) they invest significantly in oil and gas companies. There has been a long list of other pressures on BlackRock, including protesters outside their London office, nuns filing a joint shareholder motion before their annual meeting, a letter from Congress… and the list goes on.

In an interview with me on the *Energy Thinks* podcast, Goldman Sachs' Michele Della Vigna, author of the *Carbonomics* report,[13] stated that "climate change shareholder resolutions have doubled in the last five years, but more importantly, shareholder support [of those resolutions] has tripled."

BlackRock isn't alone.

Activists have also targeted the second-largest global asset manager, Vanguard Group. In December, shareholder proposals were submitted by small investors that criticized Vanguard Group's failure to align their voting records with their public climate stance.[14] Interestingly, in January 2020, Vanguard refused to join Climate Action 100+, a group of asset managers that pushes the largest fossil fuel producers to show how they will meet carbon dioxide reduction targets.[15] But by June, Vanguard was backing climate-focused shareholder resolutions requiring companies to limit their climate-warming emissions.[16]

The list of activist-targeted investors and banks goes on and includes household names such as Bank of America, JP Morgan Chase, Wells Fargo, Liberty Mutual, and Morgan Stanley.

The pandemic did not lighten the pressure. Activists pushing the investment firms decided to double down during the pandemic.[17] Even the early pandemic federal stimulus was not immune. Activists groups, including Amazon Watch, Greenpeace USA, League of Conservation Voters, Natural Resources Defense Council, and Oxfam authored a letter asking the Federal Reserve to end its purchases of energy sector corporate bonds as part of its broader effort to support financial markets as the U.S. navigates the coronavirus pandemic.[18]

Activists also got an early start on a potential Biden administration, staging protests against the potential participation of BlackRock executives in an administration *that does not yet exist* in August 2020.[19]

Companies such as BlackRock had been responding to this pressure by signaling a shift in priorities for some time. For example, BlackRock a) was a founding member of the Task Force on Climate-related Financial Disclosures (TCFD); b) was a signatory to the United Nations' (UN) Principles for Responsible Investment; c) signed the Vatican's 2019 statement advocating carbon pricing regimes; and d) participated in the founding of the Climate Finance Partnership.

Then banks began communicating new expectations to their portfolio companies, including BlackRock in January (with very specific expectations) and State Street in February[20] with their R-Factor scoring system. In conjunction with the January announcement, BlackRock joined Climate Action 100+.

BlackRock CEO Larry Fink's January 2020 letter[21] to portfolio companies laid out climate-related expectations, with significant expectations for the year, including publishing a plan for operating under a Paris Agreement scenario (i.e., policy that limits mean global warming to less than two degrees Celsius from preindustrial times). A quote of note from the letter: "We will be increasingly disposed to vote against management and board directors when companies are not making sufficient progress on sustainability-related disclosures and the business practices and plans underlying them."

Aspirational Policy, Regulation, and Legal Challenges

In 2018, I made the mistake of rolling my eyes at California's frankly ridiculous, unmapped executive order to decarbonize all energy in the *world's* fifth largest economy by 2045. In short order, New Mexico, Nevada, Colorado, and Washington State made similar commitments. In 2019, New York passed the most ambitious state plan yet, targeting emission-free electricity by 2040 and 85 percent reduction in economy-wide emissions by 2050. Notably, the act specifies that state agencies take climate goals into consideration *in all permitting decisions.*

I did not anticipate such meaningful momentum, and I won't make that mistake again. Neither should you.

Similarly, the Green New Deal vaulted all of us in the United States into an unprecedented climate conversation, which then became deeply embedded in the presidential election. There are now bipartisan and Republican-led climate efforts in Congress. Energy and climate are now a permanent part of US leadership vocabulary and initiatives, regardless of election results going forward. Period.

The challenges have gotten more personal, as jurisdictions in five states have passed some form of ban on natural gas in buildings, with numerous bans under consideration in other states. In California, for example, Berkeley was the first city to pass a natural gas ban. There are more than 30 jurisdictions with bans in California.[22] These efforts have prompted a backlash to protect consumer choice for gas; Mississippi, Minnesota, Missouri, Oklahoma, Tennessee, and Arizona have proposed measures which would prohibit natural gas bans. I expect this conversation to continue in perpetuity.

And then there are the pipeline woes. This year (2020) has delivered significant setbacks or death blows to three important infrastructure projects. In July, a court ordered that the Dakota Access Pipeline halt operations and be emptied of the oil currently in the pipe by August.

Although a federal appeals court in August reversed that judge's order, the pipeline is undergoing a full environmental review.[23] In July, the U.S. Supreme Court upheld a decision to suspend construction on parts of the Keystone XL Pipeline, part of a large network of pipelines whose purpose is to carry both Canadian- and American-produced oil to different distribution centers and refineries around the United States. And finally, after citing legal uncertainties, Dominion Energy and Duke Energy cancelled the construction of the Atlantic Coast Pipeline in July.[24]

And the list goes on. New York Governor Andrew Cuomo denied a permit for the Williams Northeast Supply Enhancement Pipeline, saying the pipeline did not align with New York's climate goals.[25] Major setbacks have also been delivered to the MVP Mainline project,[26] the Jordan Cove LNG project,[27] and Canada's Transmountain Pipeline.[28]

Watching the Majors—European and U.S.

The European oil and gas majors are under incredible pressure to make decarbonization commitments, and then in short order, demonstrate that they are serious. Key 2020 examples include:

- Equinor in February announced new climate goals, including reaching carbon neutrality from its operations by 2030, boosting renewable energy 10-fold by 2026, and cutting its carbon intensity by at least half by 2050.

- In March, BP agreed to draft a shareholder resolution to be voted on in 2021 that would enshrine its pledge to reach carbon neutrality by 2050. More on BP below.

- In April, Shell set more ambitious goals, including reducing the carbon footprint of *its energy and chemical products* by 30 percent by 2035 and 65 percent by 2050. Shell has also targeted its "Scope 3" emissions (the emissions of the products it sells), which make up 85 percent of its entire carbon footprint.[29]

- Total announced a net-zero pledge in May, including a 60 percent reduction in the carbon intensity of its products. When Total announced its spring 2020 capital cuts, it said it would not touch its new energies business. By summer, Total had written down $7 billion in Canadian oil sands assets, part of a larger $8.1 billion write-down for the company.[30] At the same time, they said the company would not approve any capacity increases on similar projects and withdrew from Canada's oil industry lobby group.[31]

These announcements result from a mix of pressure from shareholders; stakeholder expectations; and preparing for a transitioning energy future. Note for example that, in 2019, 99 percent of BP's shareholders voted in favor of a proposal to disclose how its business aligns with the Paris Agreement.[32]

Through these 2020 announcements, the European-based majors have been leapfrogging each other with the ambition of their commitments. At the time of this writing, BP has taken the lead in articulating its dramatic realignment. First, it committed to becoming a net-zero company by 2050 or sooner—and to taking an active role in helping the world get to net zero. In August 2020 BP added significant specificity to its plan, committing to halt oil and gas exploration in new countries; reduce oil and gas production by 40 percent; lower carbon emissions by 30 percent; and increase capital spending on low-carbon energy to $5 billion a year.[33] In an interview on a Goldman Sachs talk series, BP CEO Bernard Looney spoke about what the ongoing pandemic means for the future of fossil fuels and our eventual energy recovery: "Does the pandemic crisis deepen or weaken our commitment to the ambition we set out in February? For me and the [BP] board it deepens it, and it can accelerate our transformation."[34]

The two U.S. majors are taking a different approach—with a focus on R&D. In May of 2019, Exxon announced the company would invest $100 million over 10 years in emissions-reduction technologies with the U.S. Department of Energy's National Renewable Energy Laboratory (NREL) and National Energy Technology Laboratory (NETL).[35] These collaborations will focus research on biofuels; carbon capture; storage projects in the power generation, transportation, and industrial sectors; energy efficiency; and greenhouse gas reduction projects. In July, scientists from ExxonMobil; University of California, Berkeley; and Lawrence Berkeley National Laboratory discovered a new hybrid, porous material that could capture more than 90 percent of CO_2 emitted from industrial sources (such as natural gas-fired power plants) using low-temperature steam, requiring less energy for the overall carbon capture process. [36]

Chevron (along with Occidental Petroleum) have invested an undisclosed amount into Carbon Engineering, a company developing direct air capture technology.[37] They plan to build "the world's largest facility for sucking carbon dioxide out of the atmosphere, a project that would use the trapped CO2 for boosting oil production." The World Economic Forum announced its selection of the most promising Technology Pioneers of 2020 and Carbon Engineering was named one of them.[38]

Chevron has also made an investment in Zap Energy Inc., a Seattle-based start-up company developing a modular nuclear reactor with "an innovative approach to advancing cost-effective, flexible, and commercially scalable fusion." Chevron's investment in fusion is the first investment into nuclear of its kind.[39]

Chevron hasn't stopped there. In January 2020, Chevron joined the Hydrogen Council, which focuses on hydrogen technology research, development, and deployment.[40] In February, Chevron invested in Carbon Clean Solutions, which provides portable carbon capture technology for the oil field and other industrial facilities.

In addition to the majors, large U.S.-based independents are taking positions around climate and carbon. Occidental Petroleum is unique among large independents in its advanced fluency in climate and decarbonization.

This fluency is most evident in their aspiration to become a carbon-neutral company; in 2019, it even published a report entitled *Climate-Related Risks and Opportunities: Positioning for a Low-Carbon Economy*. We can expect the carbon-neutral aspiration to become the new norm for oil and gas companies of all sizes.

Oxy Low Carbon Ventures, LLC, a subsidiary of Occidental, and Rusheen Capital Management have formed a development company, 1PointFive, to finance and deploy Carbon Engineering's large-scale Direct Air Capture (DAC) technology in Texas. Oxy says it plans to finance the development of the largest-ever facility to directly capture carbon.

Finally, oil and gas companies are notably increasingly taking positions to support a price on carbon in the United States.

- **Americans for Carbon Dividends:** Americans for Carbon Dividends is a conservative-led effort to put a price on carbon emissions. Exxon has committed $1 million over two years to this multimillion-dollar political advocacy campaign. Scott Silvestri, Exxon's spokesman, said that Exxon has "been supportive of a revenue-neutral price on carbon for a decade. Applying a uniform cost across the economy is consistent with our principles on how to manage the risk of climate change."[41]

- **Climate Leadership Council:** The Climate Leadership Council is an international policy institute that is also promoting a carbon dividends framework as a sensible climate solution. Founding members of the Council include BP, ConocoPhillips, ExxonMobil, Shell, and Total. The council is founded on four pillars: an increasing bar on fee, carbon dividends for all Americans, border carbon adjustments, and regulatory simplification. Other founding members include AT&T, Ford, Johnson & Johnson, and Microsoft.

- **CEO Climate Dialogue:** More than one-dozen major corporations and environmental groups have begun a coalition called the CEO Climate Dialogue, with a goal to "urge the President and Congress to enact a market-based approach to climate change in accordance with a set of six Guiding Principles for climate legislation." Those six guiding principles include the following: significantly reduce U.S. greenhouse gas; deliver effective and timely emission reductions; use the power of the market; deliver predictable and durable results; support economic competitiveness; and support equity. Energy company participants include BP, Dominion, Shell, and Total. Environmental organizations include the Environmental Defense Fund, The Nature Conservancy, and the World Resources Institute.

Divest

I hold a reluctant respect for the growing power of the divest-from-fossil-fuels movement. When I first heard about them, the divest movement had targeted $10 trillion dollars by 2020. Instead, they surpassed $11 trillion in 2019.[42]

The divest movement has broadened and accelerated in the last two years. Organizations are increasingly announcing their intention to remove investments ("divest") from fossil fuels. Once isolated to college campus clubs, the movement now includes pension funds, cities, states, and university endowments—all making public commitments to ending investment in fossil fuels. In 2018, New York City announced its intention to divest its $194 billion in pension funds of fossil fuels.[43] Organizations as diverse as the Canadian Medical Association and the American Federation of Teachers have passed resolutions encouraging and empowering further divestment action. The Vatican called for fossil fuel divestment[44] and more than 150 Catholic institutions—including banks, universities, and foundations—have pledged to follow suit.[45]

While the direct financial implications for your firm may be minimal, these divestitures fuel public pressure on regulators to stop oil and gas projects and encourage communities to oppose their construction. They also help harden the public conversation about energy and climate further into a settled expectation that our society has moved "beyond fossil fuels."

Take Colorado as a prime example. The 2019 legislative session brought a massive overhaul of oil and gas regulation in the state. While many of us were working to have a pragmatic conversation about the important role of oil and gas in our economy and way of life, Denver—the city where the legislature sits—was committing to divesting from fossil fuels. The see-saw tips further away from balance.

The pandemic and economic crisis will not relieve the pressure from divest activists. Climate activists Extinction Rebellion have committed to a fresh wave of direct action against non-divested colleges that was slated to begin in August 2020.[46]

Pressure from and on the Tech Sector

In May 2020, Google announced that they would no longer make artificial intelligence (AI) tools for new oil and gas clients, citing ethical concerns.[47] Greenpeace had challenged the company, along with Amazon and Microsoft, stating that their work for the oil and gas industry undermines their carbon commitments.

Google Cloud received $65 million from the oil and gas industry in 2019, accounting for 1 percent of the Google arm's revenues. In 2020, the oil and gas industry is expected to spend $1.3 billion on cloud technology.[48]

Like the influence of the divest movement, these tech decisions may not materially impact the industry, but they send a strong message to the public that we no longer need oil and gas.

How the Disruption Is Redefining Oil and Gas

Visionaries of all stripes are suggesting that we seize the opportunity to restart and rebuild society in different, better ways. With nearly one-half of polled voters in the United States supporting the idea of a green stimulus,[49] we need to consider our posture as industry leaders relative to this opportunity. Political calls for a green recovery are not antithetical to oil and gas unless we define our role in the pandemic recovery in opposition to these ideas. As the momentum for a green recovery continues to become increasingly mainstream, it is mission critical that the oil and gas industry participate and even lead in such transformative leadership.

In May, a coalition of more than 150 prominent companies worth a combined $2.4 trillion made a very public call for a "green" recovery from the pandemic. They asked agencies across the globe to ensure their response is "grounded in bold climate action."[50] Around the world, as of August 2020, 109 green stimulus bills were underway (with about one-half agreed upon or in implementation). The largest three of these bills in the European Union totaled over $50 billion.[51]

These calls for green stimulus have meaningfully informed investor priorities for and expectations of companies. They come not from isolated activists, but many of the largest asset managers in the world, from BlackRock to Goldman Sachs.

To assess how public opinion may emerge from the pandemic, I have been following investor commentary. David Solomon, the Goldman Sachs' CEO, expressed[52] his view that the pandemic is likely to accelerate companies' preparations to address climate change by forcing them to think about long-term resilience. Investors were already thinking about their role in creating a sustainable society. Solomon's response? "I think this crisis accelerates that," he said.

Even in the middle of the pandemic, BlackRock began implementing their emerging sustainability strategy—just announced in January 2020—including increasing pressure on major U.S. oil companies. BlackRock voted against the reelection of two Exxon board members and for the establishment of an independent chair. Against the recommendations from Chevron's board, BlackRock voted in favor of a successful resolution obligating the company to disclose their political and lobbying spending related to climate change. Without investment, the debate about "stranded assets" has shifted away from one in which regulators will prevent you from accessing those resources to one in which oil and gas companies cannot attract the investment capital they need.

And companies are responding. The CEOs of prominent backers of the Oil and Gas Climate Initiative (OGCI) penned an "Open letter from the CEOs of the Oil and Gas Climate Initiative" reiterating their commitment to a low-carbon future and "combating the climate challenge to accelerate the global response to the risk of climate change." Signers of this letter include the CEOs of BP, Chevron, CNPC, ENI, Equinor, ExxonMobil, Occidental, Petrobras, Repsol, Shell, Aramco, and Total.[53]

What does all this mean for the rest of us?

Public opinion, green stimulus, investor expectations, and leading oil and gas companies are charting the path to the energy future. To lead or join, we will need to reinvent how we embrace our entrepreneurial spirit or be left behind.

Let's look at the investor pressure first. I thought the pandemic would delay execution of these new expectations. Instead, major investors have sent strong signals that their focus would not change in response to the pandemic:

- In March 2020, BlackRock announced that it would not cut its portfolio companies slack during the upcoming corporate annual meeting season.[54]

- In early May, State Street announced it would convene an industry group on consistent climate data in September.[55]

- Also in May, British investor Legal & General said it would vote against re-electing the chair of Exxon Mobil at a shareholder meeting on May 27, saying the U.S. oil giant had not done enough to tackle climate change.[56]

Investors are demanding more from oil and gas leaders. In recent months (in the middle of the pandemic), Black-Rock began implementing their emerging sustainability strategy, including increasing pressure on major U.S. oil companies:

- In May, because of Exxon's "insufficient progress" on climate-risk reporting and related action, Black-Rock voted against the reelection of two Exxon board members and for the establishment of an independent chair. Citing Exxon's deficiency in climate risk management as a governance issue undermining "long-term financial stability," Black-Rock said: "Voting against the re-election of the responsible directors is often the most impactful action a shareholder can take."[57]

- Against the recommendations from Chevron's board, BlackRock voted in favor of a successful resolution obligating the company to disclose their political and lobbying spending related to climate change. According to BlackRock, Chevron must provide greater transparency to "help articulate consistency between private and public messaging for managing climate risk and transition to a lower-carbon economy."[58]

It's clear that, with or without a pandemic, these investor expectations are not going anywhere.

Similarly, policymakers around the world who have prioritized climate see their job as more than implementing pragmatic sidebars. They now seek to drive innovation and the marketplace in dramatic ways, even where a pathway to zero carbon emissions is currently invisible.

You can expect more policy moves at every level of government to push for decarbonization and reduction of fossil fuels—driven and expected by a public who increasingly wants to see action from its leaders. Even during the pandemic, the "green rebuild" is fueling new expectations.

Why Our Conventional Responses & Objections Won't Be Enough

As an industry, we have become habituated to looking

at the public discourse about climate through political partisanship and (most often) our own political identity. Looking through this lens, it is easy to be dismissive about the trends in public urgency to address climate and calls for a green rebuild. These are common critiques I both hear and wrestle with myself. In particular:

- The energy system is complicated—they just don't understand what it means to want to "get off fossil fuels."

- Oversimplifying energy solutions is simply political theater. We have to produce the oil and gas our economy requires.

- It is not realistic to try to get off fossil fuels in record time, especially during a pandemic and the economic recovery that must follow.

- There are higher priorities on which we should be focusing. (Like a pandemic! Putting people back to work!)

- Economic disaster today is more relevant than unknown future environmental disaster.

- Investors are saying one thing publicly, but they are still investing based on financial returns, and that is ultimately what they—and we in oil and gas—must deliver on, period.

- Even if the institutional investors are making changes, many oil and gas companies are backed by private equity companies that are not making the same commitments, nor changing expectations from their portfolio companies.

- Politicians are passing legislation and regulation that defy the laws of physics. Why should we have to deliver on their fanciful notions?

- If only they understood… we need to educate them!

- And the one that we feel but have the good sense not to say: I will not let them win by engaging in this topic on their terms.

These are all excellent critiques of climate-driven energy rhetoric and the associated sweeping solutions. But the important shift we need to make—in how we address climate hawks and their energy priorities—is to take our engagement out of the political theater ourselves. The data overwhelmingly tell us that the public—and therefore our investors, civic leaders, regulators, and customers—are prioritizing addressing climate. Even now. Perhaps more now than ever.

In 2020, financial results drive investment decisions. Nevertheless, *two recent developments* must be taken into consideration. Investment firms are voting against management teams, indicating an escalation of interest and action on climate. And there is less capital available to oil and gas. So companies will be competing for their jobs and those dollars; and directionally that will increasingly include ESG considerations.

I like to think about this data on public opinion as a hurricane off the coast. We do not need to agree with the forecast. We do not even need to believe the forecast. We do need to take a calculating assessment of the risk and prepare our businesses to address the potential consequences of the 150 mph winds.

Right now, astute oil and gas leaders are acknowledging that the public increasingly expects a decarbonizing energy future. And even in the demographics and strongholds where they do not, the millennial generation is sweeping into power and political relevance and *they* will further tip the scales.

The Reckoning You'll Keep Waiting For… Or: When Will the Soccer Moms Revolt?

As for aspirational policy, reasonable oil and gas leaders often ask me: *When will the soccer moms revolt?* Meaning, reject the oil and gas opposition that is making resource development more difficult, expensive, or even impossible.

The question reflects a theme I often hear out in oil and gas country: We will be redeemed and victorious when … gasoline prices are too high, geopolitics are negatively affected, there's a heating fuel shortage during winter… choose your reckoning of choice.

I used to think that there would be a reckoning. I no longer do, and here's why.

- When fuel oil shortages hit the northeastern United States in 2018, did the public blame anti-pipeline activists who have effectively blocked natural gas from improving both air quality and fuel affordability?

No, they blamed the oil and gas industry writ large, including heating oil providers.

- In several phases over many years, Colorado communities have banned fracking. But has anyone addressed oil and gas demand in their jurisdiction? Nope. Not one.

- Despite years of conspiring events—from stymied wildfire mitigation to drought to infrastructure challenges—that have led to PG&E's rolling blackouts to prevent wildfires in California, does the public respond: *We had no idea that our reliable power was so important?* No. They blame PG&E.

- When Canadian oil is trading at a $14 discount because of pipeline constraints—or when California's energy prices are the highest in the nation—does the public say, *We should think more carefully about the tradeoffs of energy regulation and opposition?* I think you know the answer.

None of the public's reactions is right or fair. These data points reveal that the public—including your stakeholders, shareholders, and communities—does not have a track record of suddenly appreciating the miracle of affordable, abundant energy. (Or, to be fair, water, food, roads or bridges, either.)

The obvious response is: We have to educate them! Doubling down on education as a stand-alone strategy requires a leap-of-faith that the public, and all those moms, will suddenly appreciate their energy wealth if they have more facts. Do you see this happening for water providers? Or state transportation departments?

Look at the moves of the majors: It's standard operating procedure among U.S. oil and gas leaders to dismiss acts of the European majors as driven by a wholly different political and economic ecosystem. Common objections to following in their footsteps include:

- We are not headquartered nor operating in Europe; therefore, we do not face the same pressures.

- The European majors are gigantic integrated companies with global operations; surely no one will expect us to think about the energy future in a similar way.

- Someone has to produce the oil and gas the world will continue to demand—might as well be us if it won't be them.

These objections are grounded in reality. The wave that is coming is not about physical location; it's about shifting demographics and public opinion. In the U.S., we can watch how Canadian politics around oil and gas shifted dramatically in the last five years to see how the pressures that have influenced European-based companies also migrated to North America. Despite our differing politics and national personalities, many of those pressures are already here.

Where Do We Go from Here?

We waste an extraordinary amount of mental energy, time, money, and goodwill in the fight over the details on climate. The trouble is—we have not taken a seat at the table—so we are not informing the conversations in any meaningful way.

Once we step out of politics and into risk management, we can be strategic in where and how to engage on the details of addressing climate. We do this by being mentally flexible and creative—looking for places to find shared aspirations and common ground.

Oil and gas leaders must consider the directional trend of investor interest in climate and a decarbonized energy future. Part of the industry's business-as-usual strategy is consciously or unconsciously relying on the idea of this inevitable reckoning: The Revolt of the Soccer Moms. If it's not going to happen—and we have no signs that it will—we have to do some things very differently.

Let's let go of the idea that there will be a reckoning, and we will then be the beneficiaries of a hometown parade. So now what?

Your strategy should include a pathway that engages stakeholders who will *never* appreciate your company's value in providing energy. In this case, your value proposition to your stakeholders includes *shared aspirations*— such as civic leadership and community philanthropy. Give some thought to what else.

Rather than rejecting the moves of the European majors, we can study them for signs of the pressures on the way. By preparing to answer questions that the majors already have, leaders of companies of all sizes can plan strategically for pressures just around the corner.

This is a generous perspective. You set aside your political identity for the good of the whole—for participating and making progress. In Chapter 3, we will explore how to mobilize our industry's timeless values to build such a strategy. But first, we have one more disruptor to consider.

Disruptor 3: Racial Equity and Justice
We must never go back

The spring of 2020 saw the angst of the pandemic subsumed by movement for racial justice. In the United States, leaders across society began speaking out, proposing policies, and making commitments to participate in change.

The racial equity and justice movement is important on so many levels. The movement is broad and deep and will be enduring. In addition to affecting every level of civic society, it will impact numerous business drivers and social risks that oil and gas leaders care about and will have profound and lasting effects across every industry and company.

The Disruption: Racial Equity and Justice Groundswell

The racial equity and justice movement has—and will continue—to influence every aspect of society in meaningful ways. Here are some very specific ways business as usual is being disrupted.

- **Investment community:** Public statements condemning racism were made by leaders of the biggest investment firms early on. "No organization is immune from the challenges posed by racial bias," BlackRock CEO Larry Fink wrote and was cited along with others in an article in *Barron's* at the end of May.[59] He was joined by Jamie Dimon (CEO of JPMorgan Chase); Mark Mason (Chief Financial Officer of Citigroup); David Solomon (CEO of Goldman Sachs); and Kevin Johnson (CEO of Starbucks).

- **Investors' expectations of portfolio companies:** Like companies everywhere, investment firms of all sizes and persuasions are talking about their own commitments to racial justice, company diversity, and their culture of inclusivity. We can expect guidance from investors to their portfolio companies by 2021. As Dave Nadig, CIO and Director of Research at ETF Trends, put it in CNBC: "They [investors and financial advisors] want to understand how to present ESG to their clients. They want to be able to have that conversation. And the honest truth here is that there's always a catalyst. The catalyst right now is what we're seeing in terms of the Black Lives Matter movement and the social unrest issues."[60]

- **Oil and gas company statements:** Southern Company CEO Tom Fanning was an early leader in meaningful communications about company culture and racism. In his statement, he went beyond a condemnation of racial inequity and looked to the future: "We will not treat this as an event, but rather a long-term continuum of engagement centered on listening, talking, and learning in order to achieve sustained institutional improvement."[61] In addition to making a statement condemning the killing of George Floyd and systemic racism, Duke Energy pledged $1 million to nonprofit organizations committed to social justice and racial equity.[62]

- **Expectations interwoven with environmental and climate justice**: Environmental and climate justice are going mainstream. Environmental groups are getting the message from their boards, funders, and workforces that their leadership, base of support, and work issues aren't representative of the diverse public. As those groups address the issues that racial justice and equity activists are highlighting, that pivot will affect stakeholder pressure on your company. Environmental groups across the political spectrum have made statements both denouncing racism and pledging to improve diversity and inclusivity in their ranks. Climate is already entangled in some parts of the movement.

- **Police brutality and climate finance:** In late summer 2020, climate activist groups that had been targeting investors and banks started to link fossil fuel financing to fueling police brutality. Groups claim divesting from environmental racism goes hand-in-hand with defunding the police. These climate groups are also merging their efforts and calls to action with the BLM movement.[63][64] For example, Stop the Money Pipeline and the Public Accountability Initiative released a report in July 2020 mapping how financial institutions and fossil fuel companies fund police foundations in cities across the United States.[65]

How the Disruption Is Redefining Oil and Gas

We are watching how BlackRock implements its expectation that portfolio companies foster racial equity, diversity, and inclusion to see what pressures to expect more broadly. BlackRock has been a bellwether that action has reached a tipping point on climate—and we see heightened investor expectations on racial equity and justice as well.

- Along with other prominent investment firms *and* major oil companies such as Shell Canada, Black-Rock signed a letter from the Business Council of Canada condemning racism and declaring each signatory's commitment to promoting inclusion and diversity in their company.[66]

- In late June, BlackRock released the firm's three-area action plan for promoting diversity and inclusion. After citing research showing that companies with strong sustainability ratings and diverse workforces deliver better returns, BlackRock declared the firm's commitment to social justice and racial equality through their "investment and stewardship activities."[67]

- For autumn 2020, BlackRock pledged to assess how their portfolio companies have responded to the pandemic as well as the associated issues of racial equality. They have foreshadowed that they will refresh their expectations "for human capital management and how companies pursue sustainable social practices" by portfolio companies.[68]

- BlackRock has identified numerous areas relevant for your leadership:

  › *Linking performance to executive compensation* to promote board accountability;

  › Reviewing voluntary and involuntary *turnover on various dimensions*, including the factors that may drive that turnover;

  › Putting efforts in place to *recruit diverse talent and create an inclusive workplace* for all individuals; and

  › Compiling statistics on gender and other diversity characteristics as well as *promotion rates* for and *compensation gaps* across different employee demographics.

Other investor actions indicate that BlackRock's moves are directionally consistent with the investor community writ large. Additional early indicators as of this writing include:

- OpenInvest launched a new "Racial Justice Cause" indexing tool that allows investors and asset managers to customize their portfolios to prioritize companies with a positive track record on issues such as workforce diversity. OpenInvest is now providing a progress report of sorts for large corporations. Companies that are on this index include Accenture, Alaska Air, Best Buy, Citigroup, Comcast, Hewlett Packard, Marriott, MGM Resorts, Nvidia, PepsiCo, and Under Armour.[69]

- Impact Shares, a nonprofit fund manager specializing in exchange-traded funds (ETFs), partnered with the NAACP to create a fund (NACP) which tracks the Morningstar Minority Empowerment Index. The fund is designed to provide exposure to U.S. companies with strong racial and ethnic diversity policies in place.[70]

- Confluence Philanthropy's 2020 Belonging Pledge—A Commitment to Advance Racial Equity is a pledge taken by investors to "identify industry-wide barriers and the technical resources required to advance the practice of investing with a racial equity lens."[71]

- Business for Racial Equity Pledge: This pledge for promoting racial equity is signed by the workers in the business community, not corporate leaders.[72]

Challenges to Conventional Thinking and Common Objections

These are matters of the heart, one of my energy industry colleagues told me. *We are working with engineers and leaders who want to work in a linear fashion toward a solution.* The uncomfortable work of racial equity and justice seems far away from the practical work of getting a molecule of natural gas to the right location.

Objections to taking on this work include:

- This is an issue for human resources, not leadership.
- Our leadership is color-blind—we promote the best people regardless of race.

- This is not an issue within our organization.

Business-as-usual leaders have been deflecting this work for years—because it's difficult and it upends the social order that we completely take for granted. But it is a disruptor; it's not going away and we need to look into our own hearts and find the personal conviction to make addressing it the work of our and lifetimes.

Someone in your leadership has likely already expressed concern over getting into the politics of these issues, saying: "It's not our place," or "It's not worth the risk." Your *real* risk is sitting on the sidelines of this moment—a moment that future generations will look back on as a turning point for racial equity and justice. A lack of accountability is one of the root causes of our current crisis. And we each know that leaders set the tone and expectation for accountability.

This work is central to our humanity. Further, it is intrinsic to our shared future. As the country diversifies and millennials ascend into their prime, our legitimacy as leaders will be based in large part on whether or not we get this right. Your efforts to take on racial equity, justice, and inclusion head on— no matter how imperfect—must begin immediately. This is not extra work; it is precisely leadership work.

Where Do We Go from Here?

Making a (relatively) easy statement of support for the movement and leaving it at that will not suffice. It didn't take long for public commentators to start calling out antiracist rhetoric as insufficient and calling for actionable steps from companies. I think Andre Perry, a fellow at the Brookings Institution, nailed it on ABC News: "These statements are a sign of defensiveness more so than an indication that they are proactively working to deconstruct racism in this country."[73] You might not be able to launch a $100 million initiative[74] to fight racial injustice and promote diversity both inside and outside your company, as Apple is doing. But you should get to work on what you *can* do.

"Damned if you do, damned if you don't." That's how it feels to a lot of white people, like me, who are certain to make missteps. That's the small price we (white people) have to pay for living with an invisible privilege our whole lives. Let's get over it and get to work. We will explore how to tap into our values to build a relevant racial equity and justice strategy in Chapter 3.

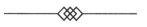

03

The Three Timeless Values You Need to Change the Game

Every leader eventually faces the fork in the road that makes or breaks their leadership.

This fork (which splits three ways) is brought about the one thing that never changes: change.

Along one path, you continue to operate business as usual... and your operations slowly descend toward failure.

Along another, you are able to adjust at the margins and maintain a sustainable mediocrity. In a lot of businesses, this route looks like success—although it really is tantamount to survival.

Along the third path, you meet change with your own disruption—you seize the leadership position. Experienced leaders know that these forks are only clearly recognizable in hindsight.

Game-changing leaders are looking for disruption opportunities every day.

Unfortunately, our sector as a whole has not been leading into the energy future. Even during the pandemic, companies have been expending valuable public and political goodwill *arguing* for their rightful place in the energy mix—rather than *leading* the public and the energy sector into the future.

But there is still a window for us to create shared ambition, a vision of the future, and a leadership strategy to that future.

Our industry has 150 years of entrepreneurial leadership in the face of disruption. I know that many green visions of the energy future are fanciful. Yet many of the early oil and gas innovators were visionary, radical, and downright kooky. Can you imagine the reaction the fella got who said: *Throw out your whale oil. I've got this cheaper and cleaner answer right here that came out of a hole in the ground!*

The big difference for the oil and gas industry today: We employ visionaries and we have billions of dollars, world-class researchers, and the capacity to innovate and execute at incredible scale. There are no clear leaders of the energy future innovating solutions across the value chain *at scale*. The public—and our stakeholders—are eager to see the vision of just such a leader.

I wrote this book because I am betting on the future of clean energy and energy services to come from this industry.

Seventy years ago, oil and gas companies were the heroes of quickly advancing energy innovation that fueled U.S. and Canadian prosperity, providing increasingly efficient, comfortable, and affordable lifestyles. Fossils transformed agriculture, industry, and transportation—allowing the creation of the world as we know it. We basked in the public's gratitude for many decades. How we long for those days!

But we need to stop fighting for a return to that era. Instead, we need to look back more than 100 years—to embrace the spirit of the oil and gas pioneers and their example as we meet growing public expectations for a decarbonized, efficient, affordable future where energy is invisible, clean, and always available.

The well-loved and documented stories of North America's first oil and gas wells heralded a new era. This was not, however, an era of linear progression and growing market share. It was an era of fits, starts, trials, and failures.

American oil's famous replacement of whale oil in the 1850s for lighting was significant, but short-lived. Less than 25 years after its dominance, lighting oil was replaced by commercial electricity generation and light bulbs. The growing successes and dead ends of North American oil and gas production and demand have been completely intertwined with technology innovations, ever-changing market uses, and accompanying newly invented "energy services" that have arisen and fallen over the last 170 years.

The internal combustion engine sputtered along through several – as Vaclav Smil puts it – "failed experiments and abandoned designs" until its first commercial success in 1860... but the car did not become widely affordable until 1908, thanks then to Henry Ford. And when it did, no one was worried about the market for lighting fuel.

This iterative history, full of grand plans and failed innovations, can guide us to contemplate how to lead in this moment. We must envision the future of energy with aspiration and flexibility as our guide. Embodying the entrepreneurial spirit inspired by perpetual disruption means:

- We accept that technology, energy supply, and energy demand will continue to evolve dramatically.

- We understand that the public expects leadership from oil and gas, the dominant energy industry, in reducing the environmental footprint of energy services, particularly carbon. We can share those aspirations.

- We decide to lead the way to that energy future.

- We anticipate the ways that innovation within and outside of the industry are part of energy future.

This is a long, paradigm-shifting exploration into uncharted energy territory.

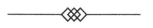

The decision to lead through disruption is first and foremost a personal journey. Game-changing leaders curate their setbacks and minor disruptions into experiential assets. Knowing that change within marketplaces is inevitable, these leaders move toward these upsets. They meet the warning signals of disruption analytically and with curiosity: What does this tell me? What am I missing? What does this foreshadow?

Setbacks and disruption spur resilience and innovation—under the right leadership. So this is an excellent time for you to be the right leader.

The three disruptors facing the oil and gas industry have created an opportunity on steroids to cultivate that resilience and innovation. You can capture this leadership edge by recapturing your values and evolving your business strategy to meet the challenges and opportunities inherent in any moment. In this moment, you—and all of us in oil and gas—also have a unique window through which to reclaim the mantle of energy leadership.

When we're not prepared for it—when we haven't yet taken on the gamechanger's mindset—the disrupted moment will make us feel untethered from reality as we knew it. The disrupted moment is like being tossed about underwater by a wave breaking on shore. What can you hold on to when you don't know which way is up?

Game-changing leaders cannot be untethered. They are the still point in the turning world. You know these leaders by their qualities. Among them:

- A calm, stable mindset;
- The ability to discern between the fashionable and the enduring;
- A lucid perception of the strengths and shortcomings of those we are tasked with leading;
- A coherent framework and approach that others can align with and lean on while everything around them is upside-down;
- The diagnostic capability to bring analytical understanding to attempts, failures, and ultimately successes.

Three timeless values are the foundation of this leadership package—what you hold onto to be the gamechanger:

1. Embrace disruption;
2. Share aspirations for our energy future; and
3. Expand your sphere of leadership influence.

We will lean on these values to embark on our own strategy.

Value 1: Embrace Disruption

Entrepreneurs from time immemorial have decided —through raw necessity, if not ingenuity—to embrace disruption. Reframing and embracing the disruptor mindset as a *value*—puts this way of engaging with the world on a higher plane. When you *value* embracing disruption, you have moved well beyond merely *surviving* disruption—putting you already ahead of the game.

When you make *embracing disruption* a value instead of a fallback position, what changes? You encounter disruption and, instead of turning away, lean forward, onto your toes, to engage with the discomfort and change all around you. Instead of the normal human reaction—resisting, seeking to control—you first relax and then accept fluidity and change as the medium within which you are swimming.

As with all three values, embracing disruption is first and foremost a personal decision. In March 2020, when the Saudi-Russian oil price war began, oil dropped precipitously in one day, and many of my clients lost 50 percent or more of their market value. Two days later, both of my boys' schools announced that they would be closed that Friday the 13th or the following week.

First, we cancelled our spring break trip to Montana. Then for several weeks, new challenges dropped daily—new COVID-19 cases, conferences cancelled, clients suspending budgets. As these setbacks appeared every day, I began waking up an hour earlier to read the news and process so many unsettling events before I had to engage with any other colleagues. My fear mushroomed into the large specters of business collapse, personal finance disaster, and health crises of everyone I loved. Oil prices went negative. The schools announced the kids would not go back. It became clear it would never end.

And then I took a deep breath.

Of course, breathless fear and stifling control are not great habits under any circumstance. But I realized: With upset and disruption on every level, my family, friends, clients, employees, and colleagues needed —and deserved—something better from me.

For better or worse, I have now had months to practice embracing disruption, and I am weaving this embrace into every aspect of my personality and value system. Holding the status quo loosely is part of the effort. The second is *looking for opportunity* within the disruption… knowing that, if you are nimble and creative, you will always find a path forward to success.

Fortunately, I have found that embracing disruption does not require full assimilation—it's a lifetime of work that we can expect to return to again and again. Nevertheless, the *intention* to embrace disruption takes us far internally. And once we have taken a forward-leaning stance into the massive changes all around us, we can work to create (or refine) a resilient, innovative company culture.

To Be the Disruptor

"Wouldn't you rather be the disruptor rather than the disrupted?" Kevin Krausert asked when I interviewed him for my *Energy Thinks* podcast. Kevin is CEO of Beaver Drilling, a millennial, and an innovative thinker about the future of oil and gas.

I've found that oil and gas employees and company leaders with 20 to 30 years ahead of them have a vantage point and resulting creative perspective about the future that we need to incorporate into our present-day strategy. If anything, they are more clear-eyed about the work ahead than those of us with more experience and less runway ahead.

In January 2020, before everything was turned upside down by the pandemic, I found myself in Calgary on a Friday night, sitting on another oil and gas panel.

I leaned forward in my seat when Kevin clicked to the slide in his presentation entitled "Oil and Gas Pathways to Net Zero." It included: reducing emissions; low-emissions LNG; and blue hydrogen (H made from natural gas), among other things. Walking into this talk, I believed our industry should a) share the ambitions of a public who wants to decarbonize and b) chart a path forward. Before Kevin's talk, I had only seen that kind of vision articulated by the oil and gas majors. But here was a game-changing leader, disrupting in the face of disruption.

Even without a pandemic, the energy system was undergoing massive upheaval. You likely don't need to be convinced, but to name a few:

- Energy demand shifting to developing economies;
- Artificial intelligence and digitization changing the oil field;
- A shift to and expectations for decarbonizing forms of energy;

- Changing transportation patterns, such as the rise of on-demand ride shares and driverless vehicles; and

- Technological innovation along the entire energy system.

Then came a pandemic, with a jaw-dropping decline in mobility and demand for transportation fuels. We can debate robustly what energy system changes will last after the economic recovery, but we do know for certain that *things will be different.*

Embrace the Entrepreneurial Spirit

Companies that view innovation and adaption as *integral to their future success* will prepare their workforce and their business plans. There is clearly no stronger formula for resilience in the face of change than embracing change.

For a company, *embracing disruption* as a value manifests itself in the form of stark assessment, scenario planning outside of the known knowns, strategic planning, evaluating progress, and making course corrections. Such a company does not punish poor forecasting, but instead incentivizes unconventional scenario planning. If change is the only constant—and I think we can agree that it is— then *planning for unforeseen change* only makes sense.

In its simplest form, this kind of assessment and planning involves the obvious scenarios: political changes, price spikes, weather events. When engaged with sophistication, scenario planning asks: *What may happen that we aren't thinking of? How resilient and adaptable are we? What could go wrong? What have we learned from the surprises of the last five years? Five months? Five days? In what ways are we blind? In which areas are we stuck?*

During the early weeks of the pandemic's economic shutdown, I learned much from Paula Gant, Senior Vice President of Strategy & Innovation at the Gas Technology Institute. There is no doubt why Paula has both "strategy" and "innovation" in her title—she must eat entrepreneurial spirit on her toast each morning. In my interview with Paula for the *Energy Thinks* podcast, she continuously pivoted ahead: "That's the right question for today, but what we need to be thinking about, is what is the right question to ask tomorrow?" Continuous disruption requires more than a query; it demands continual curiosity driving our strategy ahead of what we can see today.

Embracing disruption is the foundational value of a game-changing mindset. This value pushes you to pivot from reactive to engaging, from surprised to flexible, from scared to emboldened.

Value 2: Share Aspirations for a Shared Energy Future

Embracing disruption alone, however, would leave a leader and a corporate culture completely untethered. The only way embracing disruption works is if we can envision a future better than the reality today. Otherwise, what would be the point?

In my first early pandemic virtual call with one of my client CEOs, I engaged in some false bravado. "I do not know how, but you and your organization are going to be better and stronger for this," I told them. "Our job is to figure out what that path is and how to build it." It sounded good, and I meant it—but my gut was full of butterflies.

I am overwhelmingly an optimist. But I wasn't always that way. I had to learn: Optimism is habit. A discipline.

I drove out to Colorado in 1996 from California, and I did not know a soul. In the Colorado mountains, all I had was a faithful companion in my dog, Zodi, a few houseplants, and a pickup truck with very little pickup to it. Because I did not know a soul in my new location, it occurred to me that I could be anyone. *Anyone!*

I took stock of my physical and personality traits and decided to do a modest overhaul. I died my hair red, and I became a positive, optimistic person. I no longer have red hair, but the rest of the overhaul stuck and aged better than the red hair did.

For those of us naturally inclined to wake up cranky, being a forward-looking, positive person can largely be a matter of discipline. I watch my first thoughts of the day each morning. I make sure that there is no situation I will wake up in without an available cup of coffee. (Pity the poor hotel that does not have in-room coffee pots.) I take a deep breath and reset my mindset at least once an hour. Leadership requires much discipline of us—but the discipline of optimism perhaps most of all.

Finding an optimistic view of the future requires its own discipline and creativity. In the last section, I encouraged you to ask yourself: *What could go wrong?* In this situation, you ask yourself: *What might go right?* Even if I cannot see the pathway to success, what would success look like? When I get stuck on this question, I refine my query further: What are the qualities of success? What will I feel like when I have achieved success? In any situation, no matter how dire, you can find the answer to those questions.

I also engage in a practice of looking back on this difficult moment from the future. This works for everything from the massive (e.g., the 2010 wildfire that burned down 169 homes in my canyon) to the insolvably mundane, like when I was locked out of my office building a few weeks before this writing with no keys, no wallet, and no phone. I have been through enough challenges in my adult life to know one will eventually be on the other side looking back. When I look back—how much optimism, poise, and goodwill will I observe in myself?

Generating optimism in oneself is the everyday work of a lifetime. It is a prerequisite for game-changing leadership and the starting point to cultivate shared aspirations for a shared future.

After all, what is a shared future?

I presented the three disruptors up front to serve as your

motivators. Essentially, it does not matter if we agree with what is happening with the disruptors. It certainly does not matter whether we agree with the new perspectives now dominating public life. Instead, we need to look for fresh ways to engage with people with whom we disagree—to find common ground—to work together on that which we can agree.

Clearly, if you are embracing disruption, you cannot get too tied to *a particular vision of the future*. So there is always room to find shared aspirations which can lead to a shared vision.

While my cultivated optimistic mindset may make you dismiss this is as Pollyanna drivel; it is not. It is a matter of survival.

As leaders, we have a responsibility to read the disruptors and assess what is required of us. In this case, developing a capacity to build bridges to relevant stakeholders is mission-critical. And the most effective way to do that is to articulate a new vision of the energy future—one that shares the aspirations of a public that is increasingly both skeptical of the oil and gas industry and motivated to address climate.

Oil and gas leaders now need not only to articulate a future where we collectively recover and rebuild. We need to articulate that future in a way that shares the aspirations of the public for a decarbonized energy future.

So here's how that works. Ask yourself:

- Who are the key colleagues and stakeholders in the future we will create? Investors, regulators, community members, elected officials, and employees, for example.

- What does success in the energy future, and the future writ large, look like to them? Consider elements of their aspirations such as prosperity, ease of access, equal access, affordability, decarbonization, and increased efficiency.

- In which ways can I articulate an aspirational shared-energy future for all these groups—one that also creates a pragmatic timeline and pathway for my company to be successful along the way?

The pandemic has accelerated the disruption that was coming anyway for the energy future. In step with this, Kevin Krausert articulates a path that I admire. "There are lots of areas we cannot replace oil and gas as we advance solutions to climate change," he told me. "As a society we need effective decarbonization tools, and these include oil and gas." In thinking about a post-pandemic world, he focuses on the role oil and gas will play in a reimagined energy future. Again: This is game-changing leadership.

I believe the decarbonized energy future happens more quickly, reliably, and environmentally efficiently with oil and gas at the table. To seize that leadership role, the game-changing oil and gas leader embraces and lives the value of *sharing aspirations in order to articulate a shared energy future.*

Value 3: Expand Your Sphere of Leadership

Throughout my career, I have come to understand that I do not know the measure of a person until times of turmoil. Early in the pandemic we all watched the leaders around us freeze, delay, ignore the crisis, or focus on the bottom line. A very few quickly took stock to decide what kind of leader they were going to be in the face of massive upheaval.

I quickly gravitated to those leaders. I was fortunate enough to have several as my clients as well as friends. We held impromptu crisis calls to chart our paths and our leadership stance.

In a world turned upside down by the pandemic, an economic crisis, shifting demographics, and political upheavals, leadership always comes down to an individual choice. Even the culture of an organization is the conglomeration of many individual choices and how they intermingle to create the company's atmosphere.

The opportunity to make that choice is there every day. Only you can determine what kind of leader you will be during extraordinary adversity. To make a meaningful impact, you will have to lead outside of the obvious and stretch your comfort zone. This will include expanding how you lead, in what arenas, and to whom you bring your leadership.

Start today with your coworkers and team members at work. Listen to what concerns them. Contemplate their need for leadership. They need you not only to chart the business path forward. They need to know how your company fits into the larger picture.

Suzanne Ogle, CEO of the Southern Gas Association, quickly engaged with her organization's leadership in the early months of the pandemic to radically shift their programming. Heavily reliant on conferences to provide operational, environmental, and safety best practices, the organization had to do more than just shift their trainings and meetings online. They had to answer the unasked questions that oil and gas companies hadn't even realized they were wrestling with about the overnight disruptions of an entire workforce turned remote. Every time I talked to Suzanne, she was ahead and asking, *What will these companies and their employees require next?* Then Suzanne mobilized her staff to meet those needs, before they were yet clearly stated by her members.

Suzanne relayed to me that one of her organization's core values is "We pivot with purpose." She looked at the disruption of the pandemic and asked herself how she could use the threats it posed as opportunities, to, as she said, "ride the wave rather than be swept away by it." She engaged with key leaders from member companies with questions such as: *What safety challenges does this present for operating companies? What procedures and skills will employees need to stay ahead of these safety challenges?* She then had her own internal restructuring to do with a workforce—like so many others— suddenly remote overnight. She implemented a daily, early morning staff meeting to meet the twin responsibilities of pivoting their business model dramatically and keeping a careful eye on the well-being of her team members. She encouraged different perspectives but didn't budge on quick implementation to meet the moment. And meet the moment the Southern Gas Association did.

We have never collectively been more connected in crisis and adversity. It is important that within your organization employees know how their work fits into responding to the crises of today and building the recovery of tomorrow.

Build Bridges

Lean on the shared ambitions of Value 2: articulating a shared energy future. Shared ambitions build bridges within our organizations and out into our communities. Because working in massive upheaval is so unsettling, the game-changer mindset cultivates values that create resiliency. Key to resiliency is building a web of connections.

The idea of *building bridges* identifies a chasm or (at the very least) a divide of some kind. In the case of the current moment, the divides most of us are experiencing about our work and the energy future are driven by political identity. So in order to *expand our leadership influence* as a value, we must choose to step out of our political identity in the context of this work.

Oil and gas industry companies are stellar at mobilizing in the wake of a natural disaster. In my interview with

Kim Greene, CEO of Southern Company Gas, on the *Energy Thinks* podcast, she spoke of how well Southern Company Gas employees pivoted to response early in the pandemic. She discussed how their familiarity with hurricane response left them more than ready for such a disruption—it prepared them to think about their broader role in civic response.

Think in those terms today. Every stakeholder you have is overwhelmed by uncertainty. Look around and seek to engage and soothe your employees and communities. How can you mobilize as a partner in the response and recovery?

You have an unprecedented opportunity to mitigate future social risk by investing in your relationship with your communities and stakeholders. Communicate broadly, proactively, and positively with each of your key stakeholder groups. As a company, you do this by:

- Identifying key stakeholders—internally and externally—and getting to know what is important to them;

- Systematically building civic bridges through philanthropy, volunteerism, and community leadership—ideally, through building an unconventional network outside of your personal and corporate comfort zone, one you've nurtured over years;

- Explicitly nurturing a non-partisan or bi-partisan strategy; and

- Building overlapping relationship structures within

the company—for example, with executives serving on community boards, middle managers leading volunteerism efforts, and employees working side by side with community members.

The broader and deeper our network, the greater our resilience. We will have an authentic understanding of the aspirations and needs of our stakeholders. We will foster genuine compassion and relationships with our external colleagues. We will be poised for disruption, with diverse relationships and deep connections.

These are the game-changing results for leaders who nurture companies that build bridges.

The Three Values and Recapturing our Entrepreneurial Spirit

We began this chapter looking at the fork you face in the road. I invoked our industry's 150-year history of entrepreneurial spirit as both an antidote and inspiration to turn away from the easier, status-quo paths to failure and mediocrity.

Recapturing that spirit—and becoming a game-changing leader—requires recapturing three timeless values to drive your leadership:

1. **Embrace disruption.** You cultivate an accepting, engaging posture toward disruption as the beginning of a game-changer mindset.

2. **Share aspirations for a shared energy future.** You combine that posture toward disruption with an optimistic, generous spirit—grounded in insight and innovation—to articulate an aspirational shared-energy future that your investors, stakeholders, company, and the public can embrace.

3. **Expand your sphere of leadership influence.** You then seize new opportunities to lead everyone—or at least a coalition of the willing—through those shared aspirations to the prosperous energy future we all want.

04
Your Three Gamechangers

Built off the three leadership values in Chapter 3, these three gamechangers form the playbook for any leader who wants to take advantage of the window that the pandemic has opened for energy leadership.

The day-to-day obligations of doing business have not gone away—you still must move product, maintain operations, and turn a profit. But the three disruptors are overturning every element of your daily responsibilities, not just what is on the horizon. That's why the three gamechangers are relevant to your entire business strategy—not just one silo such as ESG.

The playbook requires three gamechangers, each of which maps to the three values:

1. Move millennials to the center of our internal and external strategies *(Value: Embrace disruption)*;

2. Articulate the shared energy future by setting the company compass to decarbonization *(Value: Share aspiration)*; and

3. Provide broad civic leadership *(Value: Expand your influence)*.

Gamechanger 1: Embrace Disruption: Move Millennials to Your Main Stage

If you fail to develop a proactive millennial engagement strategy, your company will face increasing isolation and growing hostility. It does not have to be this way. You have a choice.

I'll be direct: It has been hard for me to embrace the prospect of spotlighting millennials on the main stage *for the rest of my career.* And I am not alone. In the month prior to this writing, I spent two dinner conversations making the case for shepherding the millennials into leadership with dinner companions who "just don't think the millennials are ready."

Of course, no one ever got ready for the main stage from the wings.

Know this: Millennials are coming in hot *whether we like it or not.* They matter in raw numbers, both internally to your company and externally to our sector. And they have the skills we need to transform oil and gas companies to meet the challenges of today. We need them more than they need us.

Savvy leaders: You need to be laser-focused on keeping your millennials. Then you need to empower them to contribute meaningfully. And you need them to become so passionate about your company's work that they serve—wherever they go—as our industry's brand ambassadors.

Millennials are going to rise with or without our help. I got myself over the hump by talking myself into my role as shepherd, steward, and mentor. Once I made that mental click, I changed my relationship with millennials in powerful ways. When I seek their input, they respond with creativity, enthusiasm, and—what surprised me most of all—gratitude. Now I work with dozens of millennials, and I sense a bond that feels a lot like *loyalty*.

Your mission is to build that bond.

In short, the first step to changing our game with millennials is to *value the millennial perspective and contribution*. They have come of age. It is time.

Our Millennial Workforce: Integrate into Your Strategy and Support Their Success

Millennials have become the most important generation for the oil and gas industry because: (1) They are poised to dominate both our customer base and our work force, and (2) We require their unique traits and worldviews to transcend political risk and take advantage of our opportunity in responding, recovering, and rebuilding our civic society in the wake of COVID-19.

The best way to engage effectively with your millennial workforce is to *integrate them into your strategy development*—from how to best involve them in corporate planning to novel ways to interact in the world they are coming to dominate. Here are a few ideas to get you started.

- **Engage millennials in your post-pandemic plan and ongoing strategy.** This includes your internal pandemic strategy and also your engagement as civic leaders (the third gamechanger). Consider bringing millennials to the most important planning tables in meaningful ways.

  › **Change your "Go To" team**. In a crisis, we naturally turn to those we trust. However, there will be nothing status quo about our post-pandemic energy world. Relying on the usual tight circle of the same old people to get through this will not, well, get us through this. Every time you are bringing in trusted advisors, ask yourself what emerging leader you can bring to the table as well.

  › **Create a Shadow Board to advise the executive team.**[76] The Harvard Business Review lays out a compelling process to assemble employees outside of the executive team to work with them on strategic initiatives. What better time than now to leverage your millennials' creativity, insights, and values on the challenges ahead?

  › **Create a Working Group focused on external stakeholders.** Post-pandemic external relations is an all-hands-on-deck project. To lead into both pandemic recovery and the energy future, we need fresh, diverse, empathetic perspectives. Every key strategy focused on proactive engagement should bring together a myriad of voices to develop novel, effective strategies.

- **Use your company values to create the place millennials want to work.** Societal opposition to oil and gas has obscured—for this generation—the purpose and meaning in our work. Build off your company's values: Articulate your value proposition to your millennial work force in terms that are meaningful to them. Key elements inherent in our work that you can build from include the following:

  › **Involve your work force in innovation.** Engage your millennial workforce *explicitly* in the processes that drive company innovation. Across company operations, locations, and teams, make sure your workforce has the opportunity to inform, engage in, celebrate, and execute on your innovation.

  › **Show appreciation.** Across the workforce, mobility may be down and appreciation for our jobs up—but that does not mean we should not invest in caring for each generation of our workforce. As we work differently and remotely, make sure you are conveying your appreciation direction and explicitly to millennials.

  › **Improve society.** Remember, your millennial stakeholders are looking for *brands rooted in honesty and authenticity.* Articulate how your work, civic leadership, philanthropy, and volunteerism contribute to improving society. And, if you don't have a clear proposition to articulate—time to create that Shadow Board!

› **Integrate philanthropy and volunteerism into work.** Oil and gas companies like to keep a low profile when they give back. Instead, we recommend you make your civic engagement part of your celebrated culture. Explicitly engage your millennial workforce in brainstorming, planning, and executing your good works.

› **Bring environmental programs into the company culture.** An entire generation of internal and external stakeholders are fluent in speaking climate, decarbonization, and environmental sustainability. Instill pride in your workforce by integrating and celebrating your environmental commitments and stewardship.

- **Structure your company to support their success.** In an unexpected blessing, pandemic isolation has empowered many workplaces to test and adopt many of the flexible practices that most empower millennials in the workforce.

› **Meet evolved ambition.** Each millennial employee comes with their own mix of work and personal ambitions. Companies can reap the rewards of the evolved ambitions of this generation by providing generous paid time off, work flexibility, and customizing job opportunities in line with individuals' interests and life situation.

› **Seek them out.** Employees at every level are fighting each day to maintain their own momentum, focus, and clarity right now. It is every boss's responsibility to engage each of their team members. It is not fair to expect them to "manage up" or insert themselves into prominent roles. Every company leader should be looking for the opportunity to invite millennials into crafting the business strategy of response, recovery, and rebuilding.

› **Integrate remote working and flexible scheduling into your return to workplace plans.** Most companies have been pleasantly surprised by the productivity of their remote workforce. Mindfully create an evolved normal workplace that gives your valued and proven employees autonomy and flexibility.

› **Evolve your communications.** Companies often communicate with their employees and stakeholders in ways that are familiar to leaders but that aren't as effective for new audiences. It may be time to update your communications venues and style—to ensure that your millennial audiences will both access and process the information. Let your workforce tell you what is working for them and continue to evolve those internal communications until you get it right. Then use your millennial leaders to update your external communications to meet the millennial public on their terms.

> › **Build their skill set.** Most oil and gas compa-
> nies are mindfully building the skills of their
> workforces through operational rotations and
> increasing responsibilities. Bring your millennial
> workforce into updating your programs by let-
> ting them inform you on which skills they need
> to take your company into the disrupted future.
> Their professional growth is fundamental to se-
> curing that future.

Millennials in the Public: Align with Their Priorities

Game-changing leaders understand: Millennials now set
the conditions for our relationships with them.

It is our responsibility to engage them—on their terms—
and turn them into allies both in the ever-present online
world and in the material world.

Your objective as a leader is not "to educate" this group of
stakeholders, but to form meaningful relationships with
them. To turn our millennials into industry and company advocates, we have to foster alignment with their
priorities.   This means—you guessed it—articulating
your company's role and values in a way that they believe
to be authentic and compelling. To be effective, include
the millennial leaders in your company as you develop
your approach to accomplishing just that.

This approach should be developed in collaboration with
your millennial team of leaders. Consistently delivering
requires ensuring your values and actions are being com-

municated across multiple channels to your stakeholders: newsletters, social media, and community platforms. Most important of all, your millennial workforce must live and exude your company's purpose and values. The members of the cohort are, after all, your most important advocates.

How does this look when put into practice for an oil and gas company? It means developing and aligning the following in collaboration with your millennial workforce:

- A company purpose and values that define your company culture and actions.

- The empowerment of your work force to own, live, and communicate this culture through their work, volunteerism, and enthusiasm for their place of business.

- A strategy to engage with your external stakeholders—from investors to neighbors—in ways that consistently conveys your purpose and values, communicates your commitment, and works continuously through the multiple channels where your stakeholders get their information.

Alan Armstrong, CEO of Williams Companies, really captured the spirit of this effort during our interview for the *Energy Thinks* podcast. "We have to not only create an environment that can attract and retain [talent], but we also have to have a place where people really are excited and bring their passion if we want to be the very best." When our millennial workforce is passionate about our work, they become our most passionate advocates.

Millennials are the future and, increasingly, the present—not just of our workforces, but of our customers, of what our companies mean to the world, and how we will lead into our shared energy future. See them as your strategic compass moving forward. Let them know you are giving them the responsibility to lead you and to help set your organization's tone for your millennial customers and stakeholders. Their need for meaning, authenticity, flexibility, social responsibility, and leadership is our playbook for success for the next three decades and beyond.

The next two gamechangers address key priorities of millennials. A big part of your millennial strategy is simply to change your game.

Gamechanger 2: Share Aspirations and Set Your Compass to Decarbonization

Yes, you are in the oil and gas business. Even so, every company needs to be able to articulate their role in a decarbonizing energy future. If your investors have not asked you for your stance, a permitting agency will. This gamechanger keeps you ahead of the public pressure that is on its way or had already arrived. There are five steps to preparing your company and leadership team to share aspirations with the stakeholders critical to your company success.

- Speak climate fluently;
- Share aspirations for a decarbonized energy future;
- Embrace skepticism;

- Build internal alignment; and
- Take a public position.

Speak Climate Fluently

Your regulators, stakeholders, customers, communities, and shareholders are participating in this new climate-dominated conversation. Even in places once friendly to oil and gas, such as my home state of Colorado, you cannot talk about energy development or operations without entering—willingly or not—a conversation about climate. If members of your team do not understand how to do this constructively and proactively, you will all be on your heels.

Companies can prepare their teams by building these steps into your internal conversations and culture:

- **Seek to understand.** Your stakeholders hold a variety of opinions about climate and the future of energy and the environment. Get to know what the world looks like to them by listening to how they talk about climate, energy, and the environment. Become a student of their perspective. By gaining insight into their worldview, you will be more skillful in your bridge building.

- **Become climate literate.** Understanding the terminology is an important early step. Every conversation about energy development and operation includes climate as a subtext. You and your company will be most successful if you engage the issue head-on using the terminology that your stakeholders use.

You can gain this fluency by reading polls about climate and expanding your sources of news to include left-leaning and climate-focused news sources.

- **Engage your coworkers.** Take your fluency one step further by talking about climate within the company anytime you're thinking about your stakeholders. In many oil and gas companies, climate goes unnamed. You can de-boogieman the topic, practice your fluency, and learn from each other.

- **All leadership needs to be in on the conversation.** At one point, the environmental health and safety (EHS) and regulatory departments took on air emissions and therefore climate. Now everyone—especially any leader who engages with key external stakeholders—needs to be able to talk about climate and decarbonization effortlessly. If you have been leaving climate and decarbonization to the good folks in investor relations (IR) or the team that is handling environmental social governance (ESG) submissions—that delegation will no longer suffice.

Climate and its impact on all aspects of your business cannot be any single department's issue anymore. Your leadership, operations, and staff need to be fluent in speaking climate. I aspire to get every oil and gas company in North America talking about climate and decarbonization *all the time*. The public is, so we need to too. This effort can be put into practice as you work toward sharing aspirations.

Share Aspirations for a Decarbonized Energy Future

When you share your aspiration for the energy future with an external stakeholder, that move disrupts the usual nonproductive conversation about which fuel has which place in the energy future. Instead, you suddenly join forces to chart a mutual course *toward* that future.

Take a county commissioner responsible for a project approval who says, *Why would we approve your pipeline—we would be locking in fossil fuels for decades?* When a company can authentically articulate, *That's an important question, because we, too want a decarbonized energy future*, the county commissioner starts listening differently.

If the company can go on, *We are working toward that future in these ways ...* then this conversation has now created a space for a new, pragmatic piece of the conversation. A company leader can explain the current need for the project and the absence of other affordable or available alternatives. And then the company leader can ask the county commissioner, *Ok, now how do we meet the current demand in a way that is moving toward our shared aspiration? This is how we are thinking about it ...* This approach does not work with every audience, but it is often a gamechanger if you can engage with a pragmatic leader tasked with governance and finding solutions.

Gamechangers seek to understand the aspirations of their stakeholders: We must find common ground with our shareholders, regulators and the public. The most powerful disarmament tool in increasing polarization about oil and gas is breaking the logjam of conflict; instead join sides by fostering a shared ambition. Reducing your company's environmental footprint and carbon emissions are topics you are already working on, but communicating your environmental activity is no longer enough.

Gamechangers take this work to the next level: disrupting the public's expectations of oil and gas business as usual. Under business as usual, oil and companies are locked into a zero-sum game, where they are either part of the problem or destined to be run out of town. Instead, we need to change this dynamic ourselves by proactively upending our place in that narrative. The most effective way to be the disrupter instead of the disrupted: Articulate that we share the public's aspirations for a decarbonized energy future.

As a stream of oil and gas companies and utilities have articulated net zero carbon aspirations in 2019 and 2020, they have changed the conversation about the role of oil and gas in the energy future—for themselves, in their circles. They are seen as exceptions to the rule of an industry stuck in the past, and this strategy is working. It is working because when an oil and gas leader says, *We too want a decarbonized energy future*, then stakeholders have to pause. A space opens up in the dialogue. This shift is where leadership happens. This change sets the stage for our sector to lead the public into the next 30 years.

When a company articulates a decarbonization aspiration, the conversation about an energy project (for example) takes on a new tone. Stakeholders might say, *If you want a decarbonized energy future, why are you pursuing this project?* And now a miraculous space has opened in the conversation. In this new gap, you can discuss the need for oil and gas today, the demand projected for oil and gas in the decades to come, and how your project is *needed now* because of how it fits into the energy reality of today.

In this conflict-riddled, polarized energy-and-environmental narrative, the only shared aspiration I have seen meaningfully shift the ground is one acknowledging concern about climate change and then articulating a desire to see it addressed. This is the work of finding a shared aspiration.

Embracing Skepticism

Gamechangers face challenges: Companies articulating a shared aspiration will, of course, meet skeptics. With eyes wide open, game-changing leaders can embrace the skepticism that you can expect to meet both externally and within your organization. This skepticism is useful to strengthen your strategy and continue to propel you into action.

Let's look at external skeptics first, starting with the audience. When setting out to share aspirations for the energy future, it is important to consider your company's key stakeholders and what is important to them. You are not embarking upon a peace mission with the most strident of leave-it-in-the-grounders. You are seeking shared aspirations with your important stakeholders—investors, communities, and regulators, for example. Imagine a left-right spectrum of audience perspectives: You are aiming squarely for the middle 80 percent. The most strident 10 percent on both extremes cannot be contained within that same aspiration and have that articulate something meaningful.

Members of the skeptical public will ask:

- Are you authentic in your aspiration?
- Have you laid out some short-term specifics?
- Will you have transparency and accountability to report progress?
- Do you plan to expand upon a vague ambition with further details down the road?

These are questions you should be prepared to proactively answer once you lay out an aspiration.

Ironically, game-changing leaders will meet their most difficult skeptics within the organization. This makes sense. Pragmatic oil and gas leaders reasonably ask, *Why would we share an aspiration for a decarbonized energy future when there is no practical engineering pathway to get there?* In our companies overwhelmingly run by scientists and engineers, it is something like heresy to create operational aspirations. Engineers want to be able to map a near-certain path to success. Game-changing leaders will articulate an ambition anyway: It breaks the social logjam and unequivocally changes the nature of the conversation about not only the energy future but the need for your company's operations today.

Let's return to the county commissioner who now shares your ambition for a decarbonized energy future. With your shared ambition, you have done more than create an opening to talk about the need for your company's project. You have helped an important civic leader chart a pragmatic course through the thicket of energy and environmental politics. After all, those tasked with governance, including permitting your projects, do ultimately need to meet energy demand. They too have to struggle amongst dueling mindsets to find solutions that work now and for the future.

Once you have shared the ambition, you have provided a pragmatic stakeholder with the opportunity to work collaboratively on a solution in our shared best interests. That leader becomes the ally not just of your project but of your vision for the energy future.

Build Internal Alignment

Setting shared aspirations is one of the most challenging first steps in changing the stance and culture of a leadership team. Gamechangers can keep these considerations in mind while holding your internal strategy discussions:

- **Step out of political identity.** Changing the game on the energy future requires making the first move to step out of the political wars driving the energy-environmental conversation. Making this move is particularly challenging: Oil and gas company executive teams can be quite consistently conservative and talking about a decarbonizing energy future feels like caving to "the other side." Which brings us to our next bullet…

- **This is not about winning.** The industry does have facts on its side. Overwhelmingly. We can win all the fact-battles that we want. But the disruptors have forced us to ask ourselves: *Is this approach making the situation any better? Are we disrupting the us-versus-them paradigm?* My answer—and the answer I increasingly hear and see from the industry—is no. So we need to abandon win-lose and find win-win.

- **Hold internal conversations about risk, not politics.** Conversations within our companies can easily go sideways when discussing climate and carbon. The way to create a productive conversation is to discuss the external risks the disruptors pose to business as usual and how to address them.

Building internal alignment can and should be iterative. No individual can change their perspective on these topics in a single sitting, nor should they have to. Sharing aspirations and articulating a path forward emerge from an internal conversation rooted in company values and driven by company culture.

Game-changing leaders can help their senior leadership move into this work through a series of steps.

- **Assess your key audience.** Most companies will develop a phased approach to climate and decarbonization. How aggressive your ambition and your timeline are will be driven by your key stakeholders. Map their interests, expectations, and priorities. Ask yourself: What do our stakeholders expect from us? In which ways could we reasonably exceed those expectations?

- **Watch and take stock.** Taking a stance on climate may not be urgently required of your company now, but it is important to watch companies just a bit larger than yours and those up and down the value chain. Shareholder resolutions, permitting conditions, and investor data requests are continually evolving and expanding. At a minimum, I suggest watching how the majors and then the large independents are engaging on climate and decarbonization—it is your best weather forecast for what is coming to you.

- **Incorporate this topic into your risk analysis.** Oil and gas companies are sophisticated when it comes to thinking about risk. Social risk— including expectations for a climate and decarbonization strategy—is undeniably now an issue for you, so include it in your risk analysis. As you do this, consider your company's vulnerability to—or opportunities presented by—a carbon price.

- **Set the pace accordingly.** Lay out your scenarios of aspirations and timelines, from conservative to aggressive. Give yourself a wide menu to work with. Stress test those scenarios with your values, operations, budget, and culture. Laying out a plan, even a three-year plan, provides the framework to build rapport with key stakeholders, such as investors. It will also have you poised should your investors come knocking asking you about your strategy.

Getting internal alignment is not easy, and it will take several iterations to get buy-in and then to get the strategy right.

Take a Public Position

As part of your strategy, you will want to make internal decisions about your company's stance on several relevant topics. First you have to assess your positions, then you work toward those which you may take public and in what timeframe. The disruptors will bring these questions to your doorstep sooner rather than later, so it's best to disrupt first by working on the following topics now:

- Your company's concern about and willingness to address change;

- Your commitments to reducing your carbon footprint—both within your operations, and eventually the role of the product you move or sell;

- The aspirations you have for the energy system to decarbonize, as well as your ultimate aspirations for your carbon (hint: it is net-zero in some form);

- Your support for a price on carbon or other relevant regulations within your operating jurisdictions;

- Your willingness to make bold commitments to reducing emissions, carbon intensity, or changing your business model to accelerate decarbonization of your operations;

- The known unknowns, including where a pathway to carbon emissions reductions is unclear;

- Your ability to make investments in R&D, partnerships, or demonstration projects to reduce emissions and/or decarbonize.

It will not be long before a key stakeholder asks questions about your company's role in a decarbonizing energy system. It is never too early to start these conversations internally. Getting fluent on climate, identifying shared aspirations with your key stakeholders, building internal alignment, and then articulating your positions is now prudent business strategy.

You may also be delighted at how your millennial work force responds. They are watching and evaluating the company on these topics right now.

For the purposes of running your company, it does not matter where you live, what your politics are, or how your peer group talks and thinks about climate. Your company is facing social risks that must be mitigated. As a result, you will now or very shortly need to lead your company to articulate its stance, identify its audiences, lay out options, and get to work. Waiting for the inevitable fight to come to you is not a game-changing strategy.

Gamechanger 3: Expand Your Influence and Lead Across Society

Some industries, companies, and people will use this moment to articulate what the future will be and how they will lead the rest of us into it. In the same way that the oil price collapse of 2014 turned operational efficiency into an advantage, we are looking for which novel advantages your company can press. This search, of course, begins with you.

Leaders are made.

As we discussed in Chapter 3 on values, throughout my career, I have come to understand that I do not know the measure of a person until times of turmoil. Each of us must determine what kind of leader we will be during these times. It is easy to be discouraged and critical. It is a real measure of bravery to find the strength to turn adversity into optimism.

Leadership at this moment requires much of us individually. But nothing is more important than charting our industry's leadership through the recovery and rebuilding required from the pandemic and economic crisis. Within the disruptor themes of expectations for green rebuild and working toward a decarbonized energy future, oil and gas company leaders can bring together their strategic teams to articulate *your* role.

Here are some key considerations:

- **Think like a community member.** Oil and gas industry companies are stellar at mobilizing in the wake of a natural disaster. Think in those terms today. Every stakeholder you have is overwhelmed by uncertainty. Look around and seek to engage as a community leader. How can you mobilize as a partner with political and civic leaders in the response and recovery?

- **Share ambitions.** As we discussed in Values 2 and 3, so much of building meaningful connections with our shareholders and communities is understanding and sharing their ambitions. With so much uncertainty, your organization can bring innovation, creativity, and resources to community efforts to reinvent while rebuilding.

- **Keep some powder dry.** Opportunities will abound as they do in any good upheaval, and some invisible risks will heighten. Hold back some capacity for further disruption—I recommend 10 percent—to anticipating what's next and what will return. This means ensuring that your leaders' workload and revenue resources have some spare capacity for the acute disruptors, such as a shareholder resolution or a natural disaster.

- **Invest in social capital.** You have an unprecedented opportunity to mitigate future social risk by investing in relationships with your communities and stakeholders. Communicate broadly, proactively, and positively with each of your key stakeholder groups.

- **Using the pandemic disruption to rethink your strategy.** Now is the time to make bold changes across your planning that incorporates the other gamechangers.

  › Are you defining and planning for the decarbonized energy future? Are we leading as an industry?

  › Have you engaged your millennial work force in your strategic planning?

  › Have you turned your company's innovation talent toward decarbonization and energy system disruptions?

  › With multiple waves of disruption ahead, have you built a system for making course corrections on your strategic leadership and execution plan?

  › What's coming next? What opportunities exist right now that we could take advantage of if we had the resources?

  › Can you narrate your leadership to your stakeholders in the terms they care about?

Tactical considerations

Moving into the practical, here are some additional key considerations to ensure your game-changing civic leadership is building resilient engagement across relevant sectors that mitigate your social risk.

- **Assess your company's government affairs strategy.** Does it foster relationship building with Democrats, Republicans, and Independents? For some companies, you may need to engage within your internal company culture on the risks of one-sided outreach.

- **Consider building longer bridges.** Get to know the environmental NGOs that engage on your topics. You might be surprised to find there are opportunities to work together.

- **Build these engagements over time.** Particularly with a skeptical audience, building trust is the key step *before* collaboration efforts can begin. This requires showing up again and again, deliberately building and maintaining authentic relationships.

It is second nature to oil and gas companies to invest and engage heavily in natural disaster crises. The pandemic is a social disaster, and we can and should also bring that same spirit to our post pandemic recovery and reinvention—an effort that needs to be paced for the long haul.

Racial Equity and Justice Embedded

Companies that have embraced the important, hard work of creating racial equity and inclusion within their organization will be more resilient in the face of so much disruption. As Paula Glover, CEO of AABE told me in an interview, "We can do this because it creates better financial results, but we should do it because it's the right thing to do."

To do this, we create conversations within our companies that include diverse perspectives, acknowledge our history honestly, and talk about corporate social responsibility. Here are some specifics to get you started:

- **Realize the bar is high and resolve to exceed it.** Read about racism. Talk about racism. Look in your heart. Commit to anti-racism. Get to work. Personally, I've added a book on racism, history of racism, creating equity, or creating anti-racism to my reading stack at all times. I'm learning a lot.

- **Start your work on company action.** Hold an all-hands meeting. Set up a leadership group. Look at your own diversity and inclusivity. Assess your anti-racism policies, culture, and training program. Gather suggestions. Then set up long-term commitments to an environment that fosters personal growth and deep culture change. If there is an organization that is finished with this work, I've never seen it.

- **Commit to anti-racism as part of your leadership into the new energy future.** This work is central to our humanity. Further, it is intrinsic to our shared future. The efforts will yield results key to our leading into the energy future: building broad stakeholder coalitions, attracting and retaining a better workforce, and contributing meaningfully to community priorities. This is not extra work; it is precisely leadership work.

- **Damned if you do; damned if you don't.** That's how it feels to a lot of white people, like me, who are certain to make missteps. That's the small price we (white people) have to pay for living with an invisible privilege our whole lives. Let's get over it and get to work.

- **Lead from the C Suite.** We expect investors to assess

your leadership strategy on racial justice and equity. That means you now—urgently—need to get one step ahead of your investors' demands. Don't leave this to IR or EHS—this work needs to be executive driven, with full board support.

- **Talk to your institutional investors.** Reach out to those private equity funds backed by Institutional Investors. They are sorting out these pressures too—which gives you the opportunity to work with them to craft an ESG strategy that will meet their needs as well as those of your other stakeholders.

Your strategy team needs to be thinking about crafting a long-term diversity and inclusivity strategy now. I recommend you ensure this team is diverse and has a meaningful millennial contingent. This team needs to craft answers to questions, such as:

- Do we have a system to gather information about what our employees, customers, shareholders, and stakeholders care about regarding systemic racism and inequality—and how they expect us to respond and lead?

- How will our company make meaningful commitments around diversity and inclusion?

- Can you narrate your leadership in these areas to your employees, investors, customers, and stakeholders?

We need to look into our own hearts and find the personal conviction to make this the work of a career and of a lifetime.

The Signs of Game Changing

Increasingly investors (both public and private) and policymakers (from international to local) will have a choice in the companies they do business with. Your important stakeholders want to work with a company that holds a vision for its future success. And soon, they will demand of you not just that unique vision, but clear investment in its implementation. What are the signs you are changing the game?

- You have decided to do the work of a game-changing leader, with all that asks of you in terms of personal risk and inner evolution.

- You are working within your organization to develop a game-changing culture, with all the fits and starts that this work will require.

- Millennials are now *your* secret weapon, and you have integrated mechanisms into your strategy development that allow you to draw on the insights of your millennial workforce.

- You've stopped *educating* your stakeholders and instead started getting know what they really care about and why.

- You are engaged both internally in fostering a diverse workforce and inclusive culture while turning externally to contribute to building a racially just community.

- Your company is articulating authentic, shared aspirations with your key stakeholders around energy, the environment, and a decarbonized energy future.

- You have taken a public philosophical position about your company's role in the energy future, rooted in the company's history and values and looking to the future.

- Fluent in climate, your company leaders are stepping out of their political identity and into the conversation that is happening all around us.

- The organization's climate position is clearly articulated for your employees and stakeholders to see—on your website and in your annual report. It's also infiltrating the routine messaging and communications you and your leadership team use.

- Innovation is at the center of your company's culture and strategy, and your leaders are applying this entrepreneurial mindset to your decarbonization strategy.

- Your strategy does not just weather disruption but anticipates a dynamic, quickly evolving energy future—or articulates why you haven't yet formed this plan and when you will.

- You have positioned yourself and your company—over and over through small and large actions—as community leaders in the next chapter of recovery and rebuilding our economy for the common good. This positioning includes specific public accountability for your company on racial justice and equity issues.

Ultimately, you will know you are a game-changing leader when your company is thriving among today's disruption, energized by the opening created for leadership.

You will undoubtedly see your competitors are in your rear-view mirror, struggling to ride out the oil and gas markets as we know them today, trying to convince their investors that theirs will be the last company standing.

While they struggle, you will be creating the energy future.

Both of These Things Are True

Changing the game—especially *this* game in *this* way, in the face of mounting external hostility and internal skepticism—might seem daunting to you. When faced with daunting challenges, I often find it helpful to keep my mind as open as possible—or, as F. Scott Fitzgerald said: "The test of a first-rate intelligence is the ability to hold two opposed ideas in mind at the same time and still retain the ability to function."

Game-changing leaders heed Fitzgerald's dictum and more. Three levels of pandemic-accelerated disruption have upended the world as we know it. Yet this upset has created an opening for oil and gas leaders to transcend the polarization that dominates energy and environmental attitudes and policy across the landscape. The world needs more energy than ever before, and there is growing opposition to the production of all forms of energy—particularly oil and gas. These two mindsets have created a situation where in fact *two opposing ideas are both true*. This dichotomy isn't an obstacle—it creates the opportunity for us to lead into the energy future.

Facing the disruptions head on is the first step. Once we have looked into the face of the rise of the millennials, the ways in which environmental activism has pushed mainstream levers, and how expectations for racial equity and justice will continue to advance—we can assess with dignity and dispassion how to chart a path forward.

As timeless as Fitzgerald's quote, our industry's entrepreneurial spirit provides insight into values that can be our guide. We can no longer be tossed about, disrupted and reactive. Instead, we each have to make the decision to turn within and summon what we need to rise to our best. Three values—embrace disruption, share aspirations, and expand our circle of influence—can fuel our work at changing the game. We move from defense into offense—aggressively, but with a generous spirit, poised to lead not just our colleagues but our stakeholders and society into the uncertainty ahead.

And now you, the game-changing leader, have the real work ahead—the actions that demark a paradigm shift. We are no longer reacting, but setting the field of engagement, even while seeming—to the uninitiated—to be ceding the game. In actuality, we embrace a new stance to start a new conversation. This begins with our millennials. We create the conditions to move them to the center of our internal and external conversations. Then we do the challenging internal company work to articulate a shared energy future with our most important stakeholders.

Finally—and most importantly—we lead. We lead our companies, our communities, and our country into the next chapter. Not since the Great Depression has there been such a widespread need globally to rebuild our economy and our civic society. By leading with shared aspirations, we chart a different—and perhaps unexpected—course for our companies and our industries. But the course is one oil and gas leaders have always charted for our society: building a shared future that matters. Go claim that mantle of leadership again.

Acknowledgments

The *Gamechanger's Playbook* came together in record time (two months!) only because I work with a team that slays challenges with zest. Thank you first to Lindsey Gage, who makes all things Adamantine possible—including this book. So much gratitude goes out to Bob Lalasz, who has a way of making "writing a little playbook" sound easy and then keeps the relentless good ideas coming, until you are (or in this case I am) buried up to your neck in chapters and it's too late to turn back. I am so lucky to work with Anne Carto, who laughed when I said I wouldn't have any more crazy ideas that would add to our workload in 2020, and then covered my share so I could get this book to you. Sheila McMillen has edited with flawless care and attention. Mary Kate Dick has made this a thing of beauty. Thanks to you both.

My boys, Carter and Alec, thank you for giving me purpose in working to craft our shared energy future—which will be yours soon enough. My husband, Brian—how you managed not to roll your eyes when I explained I was "scaling back" my work and "writing a book" in the same breath, I will never fathom. Yet I am nevertheless eternally grateful. For you.

About the Author

Tisha Schuller founded Adamantine Energy to future-proof energy businesses against rising social risk. Tisha consults private clients from Fortune 500 energy companies to nonprofit environmental organizations in energy policy, business strategy, politics, and community engagement. She also serves as the Strategic Advisor for Stanford University's Natural Gas Initiative. Previously, Tisha served as President & CEO of the Colorado Oil & Gas Association and as Principal and Vice President with Tetra Tech, a national environmental consulting and engineering firm. She has a B.S. from Stanford University. Tisha serves on many academic and nonprofit boards including The Breakthrough Institute, The Energy for Growth Hub, The Denver Museum of Nature & Science Institute Strategic Council, and she is a member of the National Petroleum Council, an advisory board to the Secretary of Energy under both the Obama and Trump administrations. Tisha's first book, *Accidentally Adamant*, was published in 2018. Tisha authors a weekly series entitled *Both of These Things Are True* and hosts the *Energy Thinks* podcast.

Endnotes

1. US Census Bureau. (2020). American Community Survey (ACS). The United States Census Bureau. https://www.census.gov/programs-surveys/acs

2. Adamantine Energy. (2020, January). Will Texas Ban Fracking in 10 Years? Adamantine Energy. https://energythinks.com/wp-content/uploads/2020/02/will-texas-ban-fracking.pdf

3. Adamantine Energy. (2020, January). Will Texas Ban Fracking in 10 Years? Adamantine Energy. https://energythinks.com/wp-content/uploads/2020/02/will-texas-ban-fracking.pdf

4. Miles, K. (2020, April 08). Political Party Affiliation for Millennials versus Baby Boomers. Retrieved September 10, 2020. https://gobranded.com/political-party-affiliation-millennials-versus-baby-boomers/

5. Adamantine Energy. (2020, January). Will Texas Ban Fracking in 10 Years? Adamantine Energy. https://energythinks.com/wp-content/uploads/2020/02/will-texas-ban-fracking.pdf

6. Parker, K. (2020, May 30). Generation Z Looks a Lot Like-

Millennials on Key Social and Political Issues. Pew Research Center. https://www.pewsocialtrends.org/2019/01/17/generation-z-looks-a-lot-like-millennials-on-key-social-and-political-issues/

7.   Gallup, Inc. (2019, December 12). How Millennials Want to Work and Live. Gallup. https://www.gallup.com/workplace/238073/millennials-work-live.aspx

8.   The Deloitte Global Millennial Survey 2020. (2020, July 21). Deloitte. https://www2.deloitte.com/global/en/pages/about-deloitte/articles/millennialsurvey.html

9.   The Deloitte Global Millennial Survey 2020. (2020b, July 21). Deloitte. https://www2.deloitte.com/global/en/pages/about-deloitte/articles/millennialsurvey.html

10. Gallup, Inc. (2019b, December 12). How Millennials Want to Work and Live. Gallup. https://www.gallup.com/workplace/238073/millennials-work-live.aspx

11. More Americans say climate change is a major threat than did so in 2009, but the increased concern is concentrated among Democrats. (2020, April 15). Pew Research Center. https://www.pewresearch.org/fact-tank/2020/04/16/u-s-concern-about-climate-change-is-rising-but-mainly-among-democrats/ft_2020-04-16_climatechangeupdate_01/

12. McCarthy, J. (2019, March 22). Most Americans Support Reducing Fossil Fuel Use. Gallup. https://news.gallup.com/poll/248006/americans-support-reducingfossil-fuel.aspx

13. Della Vigna, M., Stavrinou, Z., & Gandolfi, A. (2020, June 16). Carbonomics. Goldman Sachs. https://www.goldmansachs.com/insights/pages/gs-research/carbonomics-green-engine-of-economic-recovery-f/report.pdf

14. Chasen, E. (2019, December 13). BlackRock, Vanguard Face Shareholder Rebuke Over Climate Votes. Bloomberg. https://www.bloomberg.com/tosv2.html?vid=&uuid=ce6d83c0-e3b

9-11ea-a000-77691c828ec0&url=L25ld3MvYXJ0aWNsZXM-
vMjAxOS0xMi0xMy9ibGFja3JvY2stdmFuZ3VhcmQtZm-
FjZS1zaGFyZWhvbGRlci1yZWJJa2Utb3Zlci1jbGltYXRlLXZ-
vdGVz

15. Jolly, J. (2020, January 14). Vanguard refuses to sign up to climate crisis commitment. The Guardian. https://www.theguardian.com/environment/2020/jan/13/vanguard-refuses-to-sign-up-to-climate-crisis-commitment

16. Kerber, R. (2020, June 18). Exclusive: Vanguard names names and backs some calls for climate steps. Reuters. https://www.reuters.com/article/us-climatechange-vanguard-exclusive/exclusive-vanguard-names-names-and-backs-some-calls-for-climate-steps-idUSKBN23P1T1

17. Problem, B. B. (2020). Updates. BlackRocksBigProblem. https://www.blackrocksbigproblem.com/updates

18. Derby, M. S. (2020, July 30). Environmental Groups Urge Fed to End Energy Bond Buying. Wall Street Journal. https://www.wsj.com/articles/environmental-groups-urge-fed-to-end-energy-bond-buying-11596121200

19. Geman, B. (2020, August 11). The Democratic fight to shape Biden's climate policy. Axios. https://www.axios.com/biden-climate-policy-moderate-progressive-battle-f1f13652-2381-4c20-b4c7-e4f5e33487a2.html

20. CEO Letter to Board Members Concerning 2020 Proxy Voting Agenda. (2020, February 3). The Harvard Law School Forum on Corporate Governance. https://corpgov.law.harvard.edu/2020/02/03/ceo-letter-to-board-members-concerning-2020-proxy-voting-agenda/

21. Fink, L. (2020, July 14). Larry Fink's Letter to CEOs. BlackRock. https://www.blackrock.com/corporate/investor-relations/larry-fink-ceo-letter

22. California's Cities Lead the Way to a Gas-Free Future. (2020,

September 14). Sierra Club. https://www.sierraclub.org/articles/2020/07/californias-cities-lead-way-gas-free-future

23. MacPHERSON, J. (2020, August 5). Court reverses order to shut down Dakota Access pipeline. Star Tribune. https://www.startribune.com/court-reverses-order-to-shut-down-dakota-access-pipeline/572019052/?refresh=true

24. Dominion Energy and Duke Energy Cancel the Atlantic Coast Pipeline. (2016, August 1). Atlantic Coast Pipeline. https://atlanticcoastpipeline.com/news/2020/7/5/dominion-energy-and-duke-energy-cancel-the-atlantic-coast-pipeline.aspx

25. French, M. J. (2020, May 15). Cuomo administration cites new climate law in denying controversial New York, New Jersey pipeline. Politico. https://www.politico.com/states/new-york/albany/story/2020/05/15/cuomo-administration-cites-new-climate-law-in-denying-controversial-new-york-new-jersey-pipeline-1284299

26. Sorg, L. (2020, August 12). BREAKING: DEQ denies key permits for MVP Southgate natural gas pipeline. NC Policy Watch. https://www.ncpolicywatch.com/2020/08/11/breaking-deq-denies-key-permits-for-mvp-southgate-natural-gas-pipeline/

27. Oregon agency delivers setback to Jordan Cove LNG terminal project. (2020). KDRV News. https://www.kdrv.com/content/news/Oregon-agency-delivers-setback-to-Jordan-Cove-terminal-project-571854201.html

28. Cunningham, N. (2020, July 23). Canada's TransMountain Pipeline Faces Another Major Setback. OilPrice.Com. https://oilprice.com/Energy/Energy-General/Canadas-TransMountain-Pipeline-Faces-Another-Major-Setback.html

29. Parnell, J. (2020, April 16). Shell sets net-zero target for 2050, emphasizing power and renewables. Green Tech Media. https://www.greentechmedia.com/articles/read/shell-to-trigger-power-and-renewables-growth-for-new-net-zero-push

30. Herron, J. (2020, July 29). Total writes down $7 billion of Canadian oil sands assets in decarbonization push. World Oil. https://www.worldoil.com/news/2020/7/29/total-writes-down-7-billion-of-canadian-oil-sands-assets-in-decarbonization-push

31. Journal, W. (2020, May 5). Total Pledges Net-Zero Emissions by 2050. Wall Street Journal. https://www.wsj.com/articles/total-pledges-net-zero-emissions-by-2050-11588704472

32. Pontecorvo, E. (2020, June 1). Shareholders to Big Oil: Do more on climate change. Grist. https://grist.org/climate/shareholders-to-big-oil-do-more-on-climate-change/

33. Geman, B. (2020, August 4). Axios Generate. Axios. https://www.axios.com/newsletters/axios-generate-0e908f6a-cd6c-41b8-974f-cda9daf75aee.html

34. Bernard Looney, Chief Executive Officer of BP. (2020, May 12). [Video]. YouTube. https://www.youtube.com/watch?v=0W-WxsYy_Kqw

35. ExxonMobil Partnership Will Support National Lab Research for Future Energy Solutions at Scale. (2019, May 8). NREL. https://www.nrel.gov/news/program/2019/exxonmobil-partnership-will-support-national-lab-research-for-future-energy-solutions-at-scale.html

36. ExxonMobil Collaborates on Discovery of New Material to Enhance Carbon Capture Technology. (2020, July 24). Business Wire.

37. https://www.businesswire.com/news/home/20200724005048/en/ExxonMobil-Collaborates-Discovery-New-Material-Enhance-Carbon

38. Geman, B. (2019, May 22). A new project to suck CO2 from the sky. Axios. https://www.axios.com/new-project-suck-co2-sky-fc57fd9f-310d-4c96-b6fd-04d96a24ba40.html

39. CE Named a 2020 World Economic Forum Technology Pio-

neer. (2020, June 16). Carbon Engineering. https://carbonengineering.com/news-updates/ce-technology-pioneer/

40. Chevron. (2020). Press Releases. https://www.chevron.com/investors/press-releases

41. Chevron Joins Hydrogen Council. (2020). Chevron Corporation. https://chevroncorp.gcs-web.com/news-releases/news-release-details/chevron-joins-hydrogen-council

42. Harder, A. (2018, October 9). Exxon gives million-dollar backing to carbon tax push. Axios. https://www.axios.com/exxon-1-million-carbon-tax-push-e9e365ea-23e5-40fc-9884-8466abd5d34c.html

43. A new fossil free milestone: $11 trillion has been committed to divest from fossil fuels. (2019, September 8). 350.Org. https://350.org/11-trillion-divested/

44. Roberts, K. (2018, September 11). Case Study: NYC Moves to Divest Pension Funds - ICLEI. ICLEI USA. https://icleiusa.org/nyc-divestment/

45. Vatican's call for fossil fuel divestment could have long-term impacts. (2019). S&P Global Market Intelligence. https://www.spglobal.com/marketintelligence/en/news-insights/latest-news-headlines/vatican-s-call-for-fossil-fuel-divestment-could-have-long-term-impacts-59221023

46. (2020, April 9). Catholic institutions divest from fossil fuels. Yale Climate Connections. https://yaleclimateconnections.org/2020/04/catholic-institutions-divest-from-fossil-fuels/

47. Extinction Rebellion commit to 'fresh wave' of direct action against 'non-divested colleges.' (2020, August). Varsity Online. https://www.varsity.co.uk/news/19672

48. O'Brian, M. (2020, May 19). Google says it won't build AI tools for oil and gas drillers. The Associated Press. https://apnews.com/c84ba59a7d7629cc6e1a7b7f3e626574

49. Shead, S. (2020, May 20). Google plans to stop making

A.I. tools for oil and gas firms. CNBC. https://www.cnbc.com/2020/05/20/google-ai-greenpeace-oil-gas.html

50. Kanfer, B. (2020, March 24). Voters Want a Green Stimulus. Data For Progress. https://www.dataforprogress.org/blog/3/24/voters-want-green-stimulus

51. B. (2020, May 18). Companies Worth $2 Trillion Are Calling for a Green Recovery. Bloomberg. https://www.bloomberg.com/news/articles/2020-05-18/companies-worth-2-trillion-are-calling-for-a-green-recovery?mkt_tok=eyJpIjoiWTJRe-k9ESTVOMkUwWkRRNCIsInQiOiJXNWlZU1Y3dXQzO-E5YOHFKQ0NWSlVIbEdRcjVVK2hXaFwvbjlMK0l5UTd-0STRTMGh2WXpFTW5yeEZXVkY2UkdtaVVOcEFWZ1R-wanZkc2hyKzdCOGNXd1dJcERRxd3pjQ0wrQ25PaFhnYU9E-MzdoZ01henNIcm1CbEdqV05WaXJaejgifQ%3D%3D

52. Prater, T. (2020, September 4). Coronavirus: Tracking how the world's 'green recovery' plans aim to cut emissions. Carbon Brief. https://www.carbonbrief.org/coronavirus-tracking-how-the-worlds-green-recovery-plans-aim-to-cut-emissions

53. Ellfeldt, A. (2020, May 26). Goldman CEO: Sustainability is key to competitive returns - Governors' Wind Energy Coalition. Governor's Wind and Solar Coalition. https://governorswindenergycoalition.org/goldman-ceo-sustainability-is-key-to-competitive-returns/

54. Open letter from the CEOs of the Oil and Gas Climate Initiative. (2020, May 26). Oil and Gas Climate Initiative. https://vklb72qn0p747zkmy18w0m8g-wpengine.netdna-ssl.com/wp-content/uploads/2020/05/OGCI_CEO-Letter_EN.pdf

55. Kerber, R. (2020, March 19). BlackRock stands by climate priorities, sees tougher shareholder votes. Reuters. https://www.reuters.com/article/us-health-coronavirus-blackrock/blackrock-stands-by-climate-priorities-sees-tougher-shareholder-votes-idUSKBN2151EJ

56. Mair, V. (2020, May 7). State Street to convene industry group on consistent climate data. Responsible Investor. https://www. responsible-investor.com/articles/state-street-to-convene-in- dustry-group-on-consistent-climate-data

57. Nasralla, R. (2020, May 12). Investor Legal & General to vote against Exxon chair re-election over climate. Reuters. https:// www.reuters.com/article/lg-exxon-climate-agm/investor-le- gal-general-to-vote-against-exxon-chair-re-election-over-cli- mate-idUSL8N2CU4KH

58. (2020, May 27). Voting Bulletin: Exxon Mobil Corporation. BlackRock. https://www.blackrock.com/corporate/literature/ press-release/blk-vote-bulletin-exxon-mobil-may-2020.pdf

59. (2020, May 27). Voting Bulletin: Chevron Corporation. BlackRock. https://www.blackrock.com/corporate/literature/ press-release/blk-vote-bulletin-chevron-may-2020.pdf

60. Walsh, B. (2020, May 31). Jamie Dimon, Larry Fink and Other Execs Denounce Racism Amid Protests. Barron's. https://www. barrons.com/articles/larry-fink-jamie-dimon-and-other-ex- ecs-denounce-racism-amid-protests-51590957357

61. Neuwirth, A. (2020, June 8). Dave Nadig Talks Protests And ESG Investing On CNBC. ETF Trends. https://www.etftrends. com/dave-nadig-talks-protests-and-esg-investing-on-cnbc/

62. A message from Southern Company CEO Tom Fanning on ra- cial tensions across the country. (2020, June 6). Southern Com- pany. https://www.southerncompany.com/newsroom/2020/ june-2020/ceo-tom-fanning-on-racial-tensions-across-the- country.html

63. (2020, July 8). Duke Energy pledges $1 million in grants to sup- port social justice and racial equity. Duke Energy. https://news. duke-energy.com/releases/duke-energy-pledges-1-million-in- grants-to-support-social-justice-and-racial-equity

64. Herr, A. (2020, July 28). How the fossil fuel industry drives

climate change and police brutality. Grist. https://grist.org/ justice/how-the-fossil-fuel-industry-drives-climate-change- and-police-brutality/

65. Lakhani, N. (2020, August 14). Revealed: oil giants help fund powerful police groups in top US cities. The Guardian. https://www.theguardian.com/us-news/2020/jul/27/fossil-fu- els-oil-gas-industry-police-foundations

66. Henn, J. (2020b, July 27). Wall Street and Fossil Fuel Compa- nies Are Funding Police Violence. Stop the Money Pipeline. https://stopthemoneypipeline.com/wall-street-and-fossil-fuel- companies-are-funding-police-violence/

67. Canadian business leaders come together to denounce racism in all its forms. (2020, June 3). Business Council of Canada. https://thebusinesscouncil.ca/news/canadian-business-lead- ers-come-together-to-denounce-racism-in-all-its-forms/

68. Racial equity and inclusion. (2020, June 22). BlackRock. https:// www.blackrock.com/corporate/about-us/social-impact/ad- vancing-racial-equity

69. (2020, January). Investment Stewardship's approach to engage- ment on human capital management. BlackRock. https://www. blackrock.com/corporate/literature/publication/blk-commen- tary-engagement-on-human-capital.pdf

70. A year after launching a 'Racial Justice' investing tool, OpenInvest adds 13 companies to its list—and cuts sev- en underperformers. (2020, August 20). Fortune. https:// fortune.com/2020/08/20/openinvest-racial-justice-invest- ment-screen-sp-500-companies/

71. NAACP Impact Shares. (2020). Impact Shares. https://impac- tetfs.org/naacp-etf/

72. C. (2020, August 21). THE 2020 BELONGING PLEDGE – A COMMITMENT TO ADVANCE RACIAL EQUITY. Conflu- ence Philanthropy 2020. https://www.confluencephilanthropy.

org/Racial-Equity-Pledge#:%7E:text=THE%202020%20
BELONGING%20PLEDGE%20%E2%80%93%20A%20
COMMITMENT%20TO%20ADVANCE%20RACIAL%20
EQUITY,-June%2017%202020&text=In%20response%2C%20
Confluence%20Members%20and,the%20Belonging%20
Pledge%2C%20%232020belongingpledge.&text=We%20
must%20all%20do%20our,stand%20up%20for%20racial%20
equity.

73. Business Response to Racial Injustice. (2020). Leadership Now
Project. https://www.leadershipnowproject.org/businessforra-
cialequity

74. Thorbecke, C. (2020, June 10). Does Black Lives Matter sell?
As protests roil the nation, corporate America's response met
with skepticism. ABC News. https://abcnews.go.com/US/
black-lives-matter-sell-protests-roil-nation-corporate/sto-
ry?id=71150331

75. Apple is launching a $100 million initiative to fight racial
injustice and promote diversity both inside and outside the
company. (2020, June 11). Business Insider. https://www.
businessinsider.com/apple-launches-100-million-racial-equi-
ty-justice-initiative-2020-6?international=true&r=US&IR=T

76. Why You Should Create a "Shadow Board" of Younger
Employees. Harvard Business Review. June 4, 2019. https://
hbr.org/2019/06/why-you-should-create-a-shadow-board-of-
younger-employees

Made in the USA
Coppell, TX
25 April 2021

54517435R00079